TEACHERS FOR LIFE

ADVICE AND METHODS GATHERED ALONG THE WAY

MAX MALIKOW

Rowman & Littlefield Education
Lanham, Maryland • Toronto • Oxford
2006

Published in the United States of America
by Rowman & Littlefield Education
A Division of Rowman & Littlefield Publishers, Inc.
A wholly owned subsidary of The Rowman & Littlefield Publishing
Group, Inc.
4501 Forbes Boulevard, Suite 200, Lanham, Maryland 20706
www.rowmaneducation.com

PO Box 317
Oxford
OX2 9RU, UK

British Library Cataloguing in Publication Information Available

Library of Congress Cataloging-in-Publication Data

Malikow, Max.
    Teachers for life : advice and methods gathered along the way /
Max Malikow.
        p. cm.
    Includes bibliographical references.
    ISBN-13: 978-1-57886-342-6 (hardcover : alk. paper)
    ISBN-13: 978-1-57886-335-8 (pbk. : alk. paper)
    ISBN-10: 1-57886-342-2 (hardcover : alk. paper)
    ISBN-10: 1-57886-335-X (pbk. : alk. paper)
    1. Educational psychology. 2. Education—Philosophy. 3. Teaching.
I. Title.

LB1051.M22645 2006
371.1—dc22

                                                        2005029235

With the drawing of this Love, and the Voice of this Calling,
we shall not cease from exploration
and the end of all our exploring
will be to arrive where we started
and know the place for the first time.

—T. S. Eliot

To Rachel Joy: The idea for this book began when you announced your decision to become an English teacher with these words: "I know what I want; I want Mrs. Merola's job!"

To Rabbi Earl Grollman: there could be no second book without a first one. Because of you, there was a first one.

CONTENTS

CONTENTS

ACKNOWLEDGMENTS

I have accumulated considerable debt in the writing of this book. I am indebted to Thomas Lickona for the time he gave to a careful reading of my manuscript. His insightful remarks demonstrated his excellent scholarship; his encouraging words demonstrated his kindness. I owe a debt of gratitude to Steve Fleury for his sincere interest in my ideas. The word *thoughtful* has two definitions; it can mean either considerate or contemplative. Steve is thoughtful in both senses of the word. My colleagues Robert Anderson, Antonio Eppolito, Norb Henry, Cathy Leogrande, and Patricia Ruggerio-Schmidt were unstintingly available to me. In the years ahead I hope to repay them for their efforts on my behalf. There is huge indebtedness to my typist, Tracy Brown, who never lost patience with me through months of revisions and revisions of revisions. Finally, I am obligated to Tom Koerner, vice president and editorial director of Rowman & Littlefield Education, who decided my ideas merited publication.

FOREWORD

This is not your ordinary book about teaching. To be sure, there's lots of nuts-and-bolts advice on every facet of being a teacher, from examining your own motivation to teach to planning effective lessons, meeting the needs of diverse learners, constructing a good test, and dealing with difficult parents. But there's much more: inspiring quotes at the start of every chapter, real tasks to do (as much fun as a crossword puzzle), cross-cultural wisdom, humor that will make you laugh out loud, vivid anecdotes from many realms of experience beyond the world of education, and stories from the author's own life. This is a kind of *Tuesdays with Morrie* for teachers-to-be—actually, for all of us who spend our life in the humbling enterprise of trying to help others learn. Max Malikow reminds us that this is a high calling, worthy of the very best we can give.

Tom Lickona
Author of *Character Matters* and director of
the Center for the 4th and 5th Rs

INTRODUCTION

The best-educated human being is the one who understands most about the life in which he is placed.

—Helen Keller

You've decided to be a teacher and you're somewhere in the process of preparing for this work. Or perhaps you've finished your education and soon will begin your first teaching assignment. This book expresses my effort to anticipate and address issues you're likely to face as a beginning teacher. This book provides a review of some things you've been taught, a preview of things you're likely to encounter, and compensation for still other things you should have been taught but weren't.

My thirty years of teaching, which includes teaching teachers how to teach, gives me confidence that these pages contain thoughts and suggestions that will be helpful to you. But this book doesn't come from my experience alone. As a professor of education, I am familiar with educational research and the collective experience of countless teachers. Thus what you'll be reading comes from hundreds of years of teaching thousands of students.

Before you go out to teach, we'd like you to know some things because they've worked for us. I've written in the spirit of these words of the German philosopher Friedrich Nietzsche: "An educator never says what he himself thinks, but only that which he thinks it is good for those whom he is educating to hear" (Kelly-Gangi and Patterson 2001).

1

WHAT DOES IT MEAN TO LEARN SOMETHING?

Education is the ability to listen to almost anything without losing your temper or your self-confidence.

—Robert Frost

THE TEN FOODS EXERCISE

Here's a list for you to consider:

1. Broccoli
2. Blueberries
3. Garlic
4. Green tea
5. Nuts
6. Oats
7. Red wine
8. Salmon

9. Spinach
10. Tomatoes

Take a couple of minutes to answer this question: What is the above list?

As you attempted to answer this question, you engaged in a learning experience. One description of learning is as an effort to make sense of something.

The answer to the question is that it's a list of the ten foods nutritionists agree should be part of a healthy diet (Horowitz 2003). (Nutritionists also agree that french fries ought to be eliminated from everybody's diet. Sorry about that.)

Given what you've just read and assuming this is new information for you, here's another question: Have you learned something? If the reception of new information constitutes learning, then you've just learned something. However, if learning is defined as *any experience that results in a relatively permanent change in behavior,* then you've learned nothing until these foods are integrated into your diet. One way of understanding learning is that it is intellectual mastery: the acquisition of knowledge. A more ambitious understanding of learning is that it has consequences for one's behavior. Well-known educational psychologist Howard Gardner defines understanding as more than memorizing and retelling something in your own words. For him, understanding is the capacity to take knowledge, skills, and concepts and apply them to a new situation (Woolfolk 2004).

LEARNING DEFINED

As a teacher you have to consider what learning means to you. Does learning include Gardner's description of understanding?

Your concept of learning will determine your expectations for your students and yourself. Teaching and learning are two sides of the same coin; when one is occurring, so is the other.

If you determine that behavioral change is a necessary part of learning, then be mindful that such change does not come easily. As an illustration, put this book down and fold your arms across your chest. Wasn't that easy? Now fold your arms again, but this time doing so the opposite way. The awkwardness you experienced is the uneasiness that accompanies behavioral change. Another behavioral change exercise illustrating this difficulty is writing your name cursively with the opposite hand. That is, with your left hand if you're right-handed or vice versa. If you do this ten times you're likely to experience four characteristics of behavioral change: (1) concentration, (2) improvement, (3) fatigue, and (4) regression. First, you had to concentrate on doing something you routinely do without thinking. Then with the third or fourth signatures came a noticeable improvement. Next, owing to mental and physical fatigue, the seventh or eighth signatures were less readable. This deterioration is the fourth characteristic of behavioral change: regression.

Each year I assign students in my courses a behavioral change project. In it they are required to target a behavior they want to change. The behavior can be something a student would like to stop (e.g., smoking or nail biting) or start (e.g., exercising or getting eight hours of sleep). The students have fifteen weeks to integrate this change. Over the years, of the hundreds of students who have taken this assignment, less than 10% report success. Granted, this is an assignment. However, even for behaviors these individuals claim they want to change, there is a failure rate of over 90%. If learning requires behavioral change, then under 10% of my students learn anything in this exercise. The last part of this assignment calls for a paper responding to this statement: *What I learned about change in general and myself in particular in this assignment.* Intellectually, all have learned that change does not come easily.

LEARNING AND MAKING SENSE OF OUR EXPERIENCES

Perhaps in elementary school you had one of those *What's wrong with this picture?* exercises in which you were asked to locate incorrect features. For example, a drawing of a wagon train under Indian attack would include an airplane flying over or two suns in the sky. Another way of understanding learning is that it is the ongoing attempt to make sense of experiences. This *What's wrong with this picture?* phenomenon was a part of the 9/11 terrorist attack on the World Trade Center. A word used by many people to describe their reaction to seeing airplanes protruding from the Twin Towers was *surreal.* This word suggests the time lapse between sensing (seeing) and perceiving (bringing meaning to what has been seen).

Humorous examples of making sense of new experiences can be found in the book *Children's Letters to God* by Stuart Hample and Eric Marshall (1991). Here are some excerpts from letters actually written to God that got no farther than the post office:

- "Dear God, do animals use you or is there somebody else for them?"
- "Dear God, my brother told me about being born but it doesn't sound right."
- "Dear God, we read Thomas Edison made light. But in Sunday School they said you did it. So I bet he stole your idea."

When an experience doesn't fit within our frames of reference we are challenged either to make it fit or expand our frames of reference. Surgeon and author Richard Selzer (1977) describes a patient who experienced a spontaneous cancer remission. The patient, Joe Riker, had a brain tumor that had exposed his brain.

> The cancer had chewed through Joe's scalp, munched his skull, then opened the membranes underneath—the dura mater, the pia mater, the arachnoid—until it had laid bare this short-order cook's brain, pink and gray, and pulsating so that with each beat a little pool of cerebral fluid quivered.

After a month of not showing up for his weekly appointments Joe finally came in at Dr. Selzer's insistence.

> "Take off your hat," I say, and he knows by my voice that I am not happy. He does, though, raise it straight up with both hands the way he always does, and I see . . . that the wound has healed. Where once there had been a bitten-out excavation, moist and shaggy, there is now a fragile bridge of shiny new skin.
>   "What happened?" I manage.
>   "You mean that?" He pointed to the top of his head. "Oh well," he says, "the wife's sister, she went to France, and brought me a bottle of water from Lourdes. I've been washing it out with that for a month."
>   "Holy water?" I say.
>   "Yeah," says Joe. "Holy water." (p. 6)

Unaccustomed to considering healing in religious terms, Dr. Selzer reflects, "I see Joe now and then at the diner. He looks like anything but a fleshy garden of miracles." Showing a willingness to go outside his medical frame of reference, the doctor wonders, "Could such a man, I think as I sip my coffee, could such a man have felt the brush of wings?"

The term *cognitive dissonance* is another way of referring to expanding frames of reference. Psychologist John Fowler (1981) describes his failure to get a coworker, Pete, to consider an alternative explanation for the unchanging distance between their truck and a car ahead of them. (At the time Dr. Fowler was a college student working at a summer job.)

> One day, as we were returning empty from the garbage dump, we somehow got to discussing a white car that was ahead of us on the road. It soon became apparent that Pete believed that simply because that white car was in front of us, it had to be going faster than we were going. I remarked that it was clear to me that the car was not losing us. The distance between us and the car was not widening, nor were we getting closer to it. Therefore, it seemed clear that we were going the same speed. Pete was puzzled by my argument. He insistently contended: "If that car is ahead of us, it has to be going faster than we are going!" After debating this issue fruitlessly for a little while, we finally gave it up. (p. 122)

Cognitive dissonance occurs when a belief is challenged by experience. When a belief is inadequate to explain an experience, a new belief is required. In Dr. Selzer's story, he recognized this and became receptive to an alternative explanation. In Dr. Fowler's story, Pete believed his explanation to be sufficient. Consequently he resisted the introduction of the physics principle that two objects maintaining equal distance while in motion are moving at the same speed. Lacking this category of thought, Pete was not prepared to accept Fowler's alternative explanation. Pete's condition is described by a well-known rabbinic proverb: "When the student is ready, the master appears." The stage is set for learning when the insufficiency of existing explanations is realized.

2

ARE TEACHERS BORN OR MADE?

It is the supreme art of the teacher to awaken joy in creative expression and knowledge.

—Albert Einstein

Perhaps you're thinking this is not the time to ponder the question, are teachers born or made? If you've recently completed a teacher education program, you would be discouraged to be told that your study was unnecessary. If you're about to begin your first teaching assignment without teacher training, it's too late to obtain it. Regardless of your status, however, there is value in considering the question. If you've been trained in pedagogy, the art and science of teaching methods, responding to this question will serve as a review of some thoughts concerning instructional style and methods. If you've not had this training, addressing this question may encourage you to believe that being taught how to teach will make you a better teacher.

The format of the first part of this chapter is point–counterpoint. A point is presented by one who is skeptical of the value of teacher education. The counterpoint is the response of one who advocates training in pedagogy.

POINT

Effective teaching is a matter of content knowledge more than anything else. Further, personality is a variable in effective teaching. Since teacher education programs neither enhance knowledge of a discipline nor appreciably affect personality, what is the benefit of teacher education?

COUNTERPOINT

True, content knowledge of a discipline is indispensable for effective teaching. Also true, an individual's characteristic pattern of thinking, acting, and relating (i.e., personality) cannot be appreciably altered by a specific educational program. However, to assert that content knowledge and personality are the only two characteristics of an effective teacher is an untested assumption. Although personality cannot be taught, specific qualities and behaviors can be isolated and developed. Without teacher education research the characteristics and behaviors of effective teachers will not be identified.

POINT

Effective teachers like Jesus, Socrates, and countless others in professions like medicine, engineering, law, and architecture did not study pedagogy. Isn't plentitude of knowledge and force of personality sufficient for teaching?

COUNTERPOINT

Socrates taught using questions. Jesus employed parables in much of his teaching. We can learn much from defining effective teaching and analyzing the techniques of teachers like Jesus and Socrates. This is what teacher education is concerned with: the development of a repertoire of effective instructional techniques.

As for medicine, engineering, law, and so on, these are technical fields. Primary and secondary instruction are different from technical education. First graders are not medical students. Further, it is reasonable to ask: "How many medical and law professors would be better instructors if they had pedagogical training?" (It is noteworthy that the word *pedagogy* comes from the Greek words *paid* [child] and *agein* [to lead]. The word itself addresses the teaching of children rather than undergraduate and graduate students.)

Further, medical and law students are left to themselves to deal with learning disabilities, developmental disorders, and other problems they might have in mastering material. In primary and secondary education the student is not left to face such challenges unaided. Primary and secondary teachers are required to recognize and accommodate challenged students.

POINT

Would a professor of education say that all untrained teachers are incompetent?

COUNTERPOINT

Untrained teachers are not necessarily incompetent. Neither is it professional to assume their competency. The academic community calls for research and scholarship. It is not in the spirit of academia to assume the competency of untrained teachers.

By analogy, professional singers have voice coaches and major league baseball players have batting instructors. Teachers require training and maintenance instruction. (Note that ministers, who instruct by way of lectures referred to as sermons, study sermon preparation and delivery in homiletics as a part of seminary training.)

POINT

Isn't it reasonable to assume that a teacher's effectiveness improves over time with practice?

COUNTERPOINT

Improvement is not a matter of whether or not it will occur. Rather, it's a question of how much, how quickly, and by what means improvement will occur. Teacher education provides for improvement by teaching teachers how to plan lessons and evaluate them after they've been used. It is probable that lecturers will improve with repetition and research in their disciplines. However, primary and secondary teachers are not merely lecturers. Also, the assumption that a teacher will improve as a presenter owing to repetition is another untested hypothesis. A poor lecturer will not necessarily improve by giving more poor lectures.

TEACHING'S RULE NUMBER ONE

Few teachers are as energetic and passionate in their work as Rafe Esquith (2003). In his memoir, *There Are No Shortcuts*, he recounts a conversation in which he explained his uncommon commitment to his work. When a young woman asked about his motivation he replied, "Because one day, I want to walk down the street and people will say, 'There goes Rafe. He's the best teacher I ever saw.'"

He was startled by her response. "That's the most moronic thing I ever heard! So this is about you, is it? You do this for yourself? The kids just happen to be there?" She added, "Who cares what anyone thinks as you walk down the street?"

After recovering from the unmasking of his egoism, Esquith recognized teaching's first rule: *It's never about you; it's about the students.* This realization reoriented him in his work as an elementary school teacher.

In the 1980s Leo Buscaglia was America's best-known teacher. An author and professor of education, he wrote that his father had required him and his siblings to learn at least one new thing each day and share their newly acquired knowledge at dinner. Although not formally educated, Buscaglia's father was self-taught and he greatly valued learning. Of him and the dinnertime ritual of fact sharing, Dr. Buscaglia (1989) writes,

> In retrospect, after years of studying how people learn, I realize what a dynamic educational technique Papa was offering us, reinforcing the value of continual learning. Without being aware of it, our family was growing together, sharing experiences, and participating in one another's education. Papa was, without knowing it, giving us an education in the most real sense.
>
> By looking at us, listening to us, hearing us, respecting our opinions, affirming our value, giving us a sense of dignity, he was unquestionably our most influential teacher.

Who has been an exceptionally effective teacher for you?

Whether or not you recognize it, much of your teaching will be influenced by the teachers you've had. To draw the attention of my students to this influence, I assign an essay in which they describe one of their exceptionally effective teachers. The description includes this teacher's

1. Methodologies and repertoire of instructional strategies
2. Means of testing and evaluation
3. Classroom environment (teaching atmosphere)
4. Management of situations calling for discipline
5. Personality, including a sense of humor
6. Demonstrated ability as a scholar
7. Use of relevancy in instruction
8. Preparedness for class (organization)
9. Ability to motivate (p. 46)

If one of your exceptionally effective teachers is available to you by way of telephone, letter, or e-mail, it's probable that he or she would be honored to serve as your consultant. If not, there will be times when you can help yourself by asking what he or she would do in a given situation. (WWMTD is the acronym for *what would my teacher do?*)

Effective teachers operate at six levels. A part of every educational psychology course is *Benjamin Bloom's Taxonomy*. A taxonomy is a classification system. Bloom classified the processing of intellectual material. Perhaps you have had teachers who have only required the acquisition of facts. According to Bloom these teachers are instructing at the knowledge level. Effective teachers instruct and test using the full range of Bloom's taxonomy:

1. *Knowledge:* To receive and store information for retrieval. For example, it's a fact that you should have the oil in your car changed every three thousand miles.
2. *Comprehension:* To appreciate a fact's significance. For example, to know why an oil change should occur every three thousand miles.

3. *Analysis:* To subdivide a whole into its components in order to acquire a better understanding. For example, examining each line of a poem to acquire a better understanding of the poem's meaning.
4. *Application:* To utilize information in real-life situations. For example, learning how to write a check or use a website.
5. *Synthesis:* To construct or reassemble something from its parts. For example, using newly acquired Spanish vocabulary and rules of grammar to write an essay.
6. *Evaluation:* To measure or judge something according to a standard. For example, to determine that Abraham Lincoln is America's *greatest* president. (Note that a standard for *greatest* would have to be established.)

Through the years, my students have described their best teachers as those who combined knowledge with understanding and relevancy, nurtured analysis and synthesis, and encouraged evaluations.

TEN METAPHORS FOR BEING A TEACHER

A metaphor is a way to represent and talk about experiences in terms of familiar or commonly shared events that seem comparable. "The human conceptual system is metaphorically structured and defined" (Lakoff and Johnson 1980, p. 3). One way of expressing a philosophy of teaching is to describe a teacher's work metaphorically. The following are ten such metaphors.

Teacher as farmer: The job of a teacher is to get the hay down from the loft onto the floor where the cows can get at it. The job of a teacher is to make *lofty* material available to students.

Teacher as editor: The job of a teacher includes reading thousands of pages from which is drawn the dozens of pages that contain information that is relevant to the students. A master sculptor once said sculpting the likeness of a horse requires a block of marble, hammer, and chisel. Then, he explained, it's a matter of chipping away everything that doesn't look like a horse. In like manner, a master teacher's lesson plan requires chipping away everything that isn't relevant to the lesson's goal.

Teacher as bridge: The shortest distance between two points is a straight line. The job of a teacher is to provide the means for transporting students from where they are to where they need to be. Bridge maintenance includes continuing education, careful evaluations, comparing notes with colleagues, and modeling oneself after an admired mentor. Without bridge maintenance a teacher will teach one year twenty times rather than twenty years one time.

Teacher as raconteur: Stories provoke us to feel and help us to remember. One of the jobs of a teacher is to carefully select appropriate stories.

Teacher as resource librarian: The job of a teacher is to be conversant with a body of literature addressing many subcategories of his or her discipline. In addition to the bibliography presented in a syllabus, a teacher should suggest reading that corresponds to the questions students ask. Part of in-class presentations should be the development of an organic, confluent bibliography—a bibliography that grows and flows with the course.

Teacher as hunting guide: A hunting guide knows the territory, but the hunter pulls the trigger. The job of a teacher is to guide students without doing their work for them.

Teacher as activities director: The job of a teacher is to develop a repertoire of modalities. "Different strokes for different folks," said Muhammad Ali. Even those of us who aren't kindergarten teachers and don't need to change activities every ten minutes should appreciate the benefit of utilizing numerous activities.

Teacher as scientist: Teaching calls for the experimental spirit of a scientist. A willingness to try new approaches benefits both students and teachers. Teachers can be risk takers, caretakers, or undertakers. Caretakers are guided by the familiarity of repetition. Their motto is, *This is the way I've always done it.* In his 1960 nomination acceptance speech John F. Kennedy cautioned Americans about "looking to the safe mediocrity of the past [and being] lulled by good intentions and high rhetoric" (John F. Kennedy Library and Museum 2005). Undertakers lack enthusiasm for their work, expecting little from their students and less from themselves. They are likely to find themselves presiding over the dead. Teachers who are willing to take a calculated risk and learn even from lessons that crash and burn retain a joy in their work.

Teacher as master: In some cultures the teacher–student relationship is one of master–disciple. In a master–disciple relationship considerable instruction occurs informally by way of teachable moments. Students and disciples learn much more from observing the behavior of their instructors.

Teacher as preacher: One of the roles of a teacher is enthusiastic lecturer, a declarer of the material. A lecture isn't an inferior form of instruction. Lecture preparation takes time and requires a commitment to scholarly excellence. Mark Twain said, "It usually takes me two weeks to prepare a good, extemporaneous speech."

3

HOW IS AN ENVIRONMENT FOR LEARNING CREATED?

It is paradoxical that many educators and parents still differentiate between a time for learning and a time for play without seeing the vital connection between the two.

—Leonard Buscaglia

More important than the curriculum is the question of the methods of teaching and the spirit in which the teaching is given.

—Bertrand Russell

LEARNING ENVIRONMENT DEFINED

"I think everybody feels that it's a good idea because some of the kids who are gays and lesbians have been constantly harassed and beaten in other schools," Mayor Michael Bloomberg said. "It lets them get an education without having to worry" (Associated Press 2003). Mayor Bloomberg was speaking about the

Harvey Milk High School in New York City, the nation's first public gay high school.

"I've been taking all these philosophy courses and we talk about what's true, what's important, what's *good*. Well, how do you teach people to *be* good?" She added, "What's the point of *knowing* good, if you don't keep trying to *become* a good person?" This is part of a conversation between Harvard professor John Robert Coles and one of his students. She met with him to explain why she had decided to withdraw from school. Although doing well academically, she was so discouraged by the indifference, rude manners, and even cruelty of students and professors that she no longer wanted to be a part of the Harvard community. Reflecting on this painful conversation, Professor Coles (1995) writes,

> She had pushed me hard, and I started referring again and again in my classes on moral introspection to what she had observed and learned, and my students more than got the message. Her moral righteousness, her shrewd eye and ear for hypocrisy hovered over us, made us uneasy, goaded us. . . . The student who challenged me with her angry, melancholy story had pushed me to teach differently. Now, I make an explicit issue of the more than occasional disparity between thinking and doing, and I ask my students to consider how we all might bridge that disparity. (p. 1)

You might be wondering what these stories about the Harvey Milk High School and Harvard University have in common. Both are stories concerned with the environment in which learning occurs. *Learning environment* is a term best understood from description and discussion rather than a definition. It is both an arrangement of physical things and an atmosphere created by the spirit in which students and teachers interact.

Professor Larry Ludewig (1994) of Kilgore College in Texas has accomplished research that provides helpful information about this spirit. Using surveys, he's developed a list of the top ten teacher behaviors that irritate students. Below is the list with the percentage of 225 students who ranked the behavior in the top ten from a list of 76.

Students really hate it when professors

1. Assign work as though their class is the only one students have or is the most important one (45%)
2. Lecture too fast and fail to slow down when asked (40%)
3. Make students feel inferior when they ask a question (35%)
4. Aren't specific on what exams will cover (34%)
5. Create trick questions (34%)
6. Lecture in a monotone (32%)
7. Give exams that don't correspond to lectures (28%)
8. Get behind and then cram their lectures into the remaining time (28%)
9. Assume students already have base knowledge for the course (26%)
10. Require a textbook and then fail to use it (25%)

From 113 faculty, Professor Ludewig (1994) constructed the following list of teacher's complaints about students.

Professors really hate it when students

1. Carry on personal conversation with others during lecture (75%)
2. Cheat on exams (47%)
3. Miss class and ask, "Did I miss anything important?" (37%)
4. Place their head on the desk or fall asleep during class (36%)

5. Are excessively tardy (35%)
6. Fail to read assigned textbook or collateral materials (35%)
7. Are absent on exam days (32%)
8. Fail to bring required materials to class (32%)
9. Are excessively absent (28%)
10. Miss a lecture and then expect the professor to provide a personal encore (28%)

"The purpose of both surveys was to determine which behaviors hinder the acquisition of knowledge," said Ludewig. "Maybe by learning more about how we perceive each other," he added, "we can teach each other to become more like partners and less like adversaries in the teaching and learning process" (Ludewig 1994, p. 1).

One of the best-known movies about teaching is *Dead Poets Society*, featuring Robin Williams as Mr. Keating, a twelfth-grade English teacher at an exclusive private school. In a memorable scene, Mr. Keating takes his English class out of the classroom to the lobby, where he invites them to look at pictures on display in the trophy case. (This is the famous *carpe diem* scene.) To watch this scene is to see a teacher showing creativity in structuring the learning environment.

The learning environment includes three physical variables: classroom arrangement, student grouping, and instructional task. In the movie scene from *Dead Poets Society* (1989), Mr. Keating's flexibility shows in his management of the *where* (lobby), *who* (students), and *what* (brief lecture with visual aid) components.

The following six questions will help you create the best possible learning environment:

1. Is assigned seating necessary?
2. Is absolute quiet necessary?

3. Is the arrangement of desks and other involved materials optimal for this work?
4. What is the anticipated teaching time for this task for this group?
5. Does your room say anything to your students? (If so, what is it saying? It's unlikely that it's saying nothing.)
6. If you spend thirty hours a week in this room, what are its implications for you? The learning environment is your working environment where you spend over one thousand hours a year. Is there sufficient light? What do you think of the color of the walls? What is hanging on the walls? Do you have a CD player and relaxing music available? Do you enjoy plants? Is your chair comfortable?

The learning environment is the location and atmosphere in which instruction occurs. Having described and defined *learning environment*, let's continue considering it by thinking about classroom management, punishment, vulnerable students, resistant students, and character education.

FOURTEEN PRINCIPLES OF CLASSROOM MANAGEMENT

I'm never comfortable when using the term *classroom management*. Desks, chairs, books, tables, audiovisual equipment, and other physical components of a classroom are easy to manage. Students, not being inanimate objects, are not easily managed. Further, there's something about referring to human beings as entities to be managed that doesn't sit well with me. With this qualification, what follows are fourteen principles of classroom management.

1. *Be prepared for class.* Engaging lessons provide your best opportunity for engaged students. A relevant bumper sticker motto is, A failure to plan is a plan to fail.

2. *Expect children to act their age.* Children are not adults in smaller, younger bodies. "Why can't you be more like me?" is one way to characterize an angry person. Do not expect people years younger than you with significantly less life experience to be more like you. Use age-appropriate misbehavior as opportunities for teaching.

3. *Do not apologize for a lesson.* If you feel the need to apologize for a lesson, rewrite the lesson plan. Justifying a lesson to your students is not the same as apologizing for it. Nevertheless, don't spend too many words motivating them by providing a rationale.

4. *Take the "so what?" challenge.* An important part of lesson planning is asking the question, *Even if my students perfectly master this material, how will this be helpful for them?*

5. *Hold students accountable for assigned work.* According to special education expert Richard Lavoie (1994), every school has an unwritten curriculum. This curriculum includes students learning informally which teachers give reading quizzes, read writing assignments, and do other acts of accountability. Students know the teachers who do and don't practice accountability.

6. *Consider the preciousness of time.* To waste a half hour in a class is not to waste only thirty minutes. If there are twenty students in a class, then twenty students times thirty minutes equals ten human hours wasted, in addition to your half hour. Minimize poor time management by avoiding late starts and early finishes and excessive explaining and reviewing. Also minimize the time given to addressing behavioral problems, which will disrupt the flow of your teaching.

7. *Have carefully considered, well-articulated rules.* If it's compatible with your philosophy and style, consider having your students participate in establishing the rules.

8. *Be proactive rather than reactive.* Benefit from experience by anticipating problems. The old saying, *An ounce of prevention is worth a pound of cure*, applies to classroom management.

9. *Be mindful that every student has a story and parents can help tell it.* Even meeting with indifferent or uncooperative parents can be informative. Their attitude may be part of the problem you've encountered.

10. *Don't say; show!* Whenever possible, supplement what you're saying with something visual. If using a video or DVD, show the part that specifically corresponds to the material you want to reinforce. You don't want the reputation among students that you overuse movies. Use videos and DVDs judiciously.

11. *Journal your first year or two of teaching, recording what did and didn't work.* Don't trust your memory. The summer after your first year of teaching would be a good time to read and reflect. After a year of teaching you'll be in a position to be more objective about your work. Specific journal entries will help you prepare for your second year of lesson planning. The entries don't have to be long to be helpful. Ten minutes of writing at the end of the school day would be a wise investment of your time.

12. *Maintain appropriate boundaries.* You have a teacher–student relationship with your pupils. While you need to be approachable, students should not consider you a peer. The challenge is to be friendly while maintaining your role as an authority figure providing a professional service.

13. *Consult with teachers who have a reputation for effectiveness.* Don't hesitate to seek advice from colleagues you consider effective. "Imitation is the sincerest form of flattery." Almost certainly, any teacher you approach for advice will be flattered.

14. *Research is better than knee-search.* This is not to trivialize or belittle praying, but after getting up off your knees, seek information. Every significant issue and problem associated with teaching has been a subject of research. Take advantage of the accomplished investigations of others.

THE SIX COMMANDMENTS OF CLASSROOM MANAGEMENT

What you are about to read has to do with disciplinary issues and is especially important. It is an article of faith for Jews and Christians that Moses descended from Mount Sinai with a tablet on which God had written the Ten Commandments. Not as well-known but equally important is the second tablet given to Moses, with the *Six Commandments of Classroom Management* inscribed on it. (You do realize, of course, that I am pulling your leg.) Studies show that failure to maintain order in the classroom is the reason most frequently given by teachers who leave the profession.

Unless there is order, the good things you have planned for your students will not occur. Your career depends on your ability to establish and maintain order. Even your resistant students expect you to have control in the classroom. Here are six prerequisites for meeting this expectation.

1. Do not abuse your position of authority. Many years ago Richard Selzer, a surgeon and author, had a patient brought to him in the emergency room. The patient, a large and unruly man, was handcuffed and escorted by a half dozen police officers. They had lacerated his forehead to the bone when arresting him, but the man was rolling his head from side to side, making it impossible for the suturing to begin. In exasperation, Dr. Selzer sutured the man's ears to the mattress on the examining table before he realized what Selzer had done. Enjoying his victory, a smiling Dr. Selzer then proceeded to stitch the wound of the defeated man. Years later, embarrassed and regretful because he humiliated a person entrusted to his care, Selzer (1982) wrote,

> Even now, so many years later, this ancient rage of mine returns to peck among my dreams. I have only to close my eyes to see him again wielding his head and jaws, to hear once more those words at which the whole of his trussed body came hurtling toward me. How sorry I will always be. Not being able to make it up to him for that grin. (p. 63)

Like Selzer, you will regret any time you fail to control yourself and humiliate someone entrusted to your care.

2. *Don't embarrass students.* A recent news story described a Pleasantville, New Jersey, middle school teacher and basketball coach who embarrassed a thirteen-year-old player at the school's awards banquet. The teacher–coach presented the boy with the Crybaby Award, a trophy with a silver figure of a baby atop a pedestal with the boy's name (incorrectly spelled). The coach, James Guillen, recognized and embarrassed the boy for his persistent begging to have more playing time. A teacher can use embarrassment to gain an advantage over a student or enjoy a laugh at a student's expense. But the advantage or laugh is temporary and minute when compared to what is lost. In this case the student lost his dignity and the school board fired the teacher.

3. *Allow children to act their age.* Mentioned already as a principle of classroom management, allowing children to act their age will require you to distinguish between childish irresponsibility and willful disobedience. Forgetting books, losing assignments, and asking silly questions are expressions of childish irresponsibility. Willful disobedience is open defiance: a student crosses the line and challenges you to do something about it. If you're not

certain which of the two behavioral categories is confronting you, then err on the side of caution and consider it childish irresponsibility. You will lose nothing by underreacting but could lose a relationship by overreacting.

4. *Keep rules simple.* In his best-selling book, *All I Really Need to Know I Learned in Kindergarten*, Robert Fulgham (2003) wrote, "Most of what I really need to know about how to live and what to do and how to be I learned in kindergarten" (pp. 2–3). With those words he introduced fourteen rules that are simple enough to be understood by five-year-olds yet appropriate for high schoolers.

- Share everything.
- Play fair.
- Don't hit people.
- Put things back where you found them.
- Clean up your own mess.
- Don't take things that aren't yours.
- Say you're sorry when you hurt somebody.
- Wash your hands before you eat.
- Flush.
- Warm cookies and cold milk are good for you.
- Live a balanced life: learn some and think some and draw and paint and sing and dance and play and work every day some.
- Take a nap every afternoon.
- When you go out into the world, watch out for traffic, hold hands, and stick together.
- Be aware of wonder. (p. 2)

5. *Remember that your students are not your contemporaries.* Although you were once an eighth grader, you don't know what it is like being an eighth grader today. Research conducted in 1940 found that the top seven discipline concerns in schools were talk-

ing, chewing gum, making noise, running in the halls, getting out of line, wearing inappropriate clothes, and not putting paper in the wastebasket. In 1980 the top seven concerns were drug abuse, alcohol abuse, pregnancy, suicide, rape, robbery, and assault. The learning environment in 1940 bears little resemblance to the learning environment in 1980 (Garbarino 1997).

6. *Pay attention to research that is relevant to your work.* Professionals keep current with the results of research and other expressions of new ideas. Just as physicians make time to read journals to learn about new, more effective treatments, teachers should keep current with the results of educational research.

PUNISHMENT: HOW TO DO IT, IF YOU MUST

The words *punishment* and *discipline* often are used interchangeably. Although these two words have a similarity of meaning, they are not identical. Punishment is an unpleasant consequence for a behavior. Discipline is a response to a behavior intended to nurture a desirable character trait. Punishment focuses on a behavior with the intention of preventing its repetition. Discipline seeks to make a contribution to the development of self-control.

Both punishment and discipline seek to reinforce desirable behaviors and extinguish behaviors that are undesirable. The experience of unpleasantness is the agent of change in punishment. The agent of change in discipline is not as obvious. The teacher who metes out punishment is sending the message, *That behavior is unacceptable to me and I'm responding to it with a penalty.* The teacher who is disciplining is sending the message, *There is a personality trait that would be good for you to have and I'm trying to help you develop it.*

Self-disciplined people have mastered the ability to do things that ought to be done when they need to be done regardless of mood or convenience. Punishment modifies behavior, but usually only when an authority figure is present. Discipline alters character in a favorable way by developing self-discipline. As stated earlier, there are those who consider *punishment* and *discipline* two ways of saying the same thing. For them, what I've written here will be characterized as making a distinction without a difference.

But there is a difference. Perhaps the most important difference for teachers is that of mind-set. When responding to undesirable behavior a teacher can have the mind-set of a punisher or a nurturer. A punisher thinks in terms of an unpleasant consequence that will stop the behavior. A nurturer thinks in terms of the development of a character trait that will make the behavior undesirable to the student. Unlike nurturers, punishers can never relax vigilance and redirect their attention to teaching. Nurturers are cooperating with students in character education. Punishers are competing with them for control of the classroom. Punishers' vigilance for bad behavior makes them less likely to see good behavior and less prepared to reinforce it.

However, when you must punish, here are five principles provided by psychologist David Funder (1997):

1. *Provide an acceptable alternative behavior.* If you're going to threaten students with a punishment, also provide an alternative behavior with a reward.
2. *Be specific about the behavior and the punishment.* Don't punish a student for being bad or uncooperative. Instead, be specific about the student's actions that were bad or uncooperative. Further, to determine the punishment in the moment of the misbehavior would be reactive and influenced by emotion, likely anger. Instead, be deliberate about pun-

ishment by having carefully considered penalties unconta-
minated by intense emotion.

3. *Timing and consistency are imperative.* Dr. Funder (1997) has
written, "To be most effective—or to be effective at all— a
punishment needs to be applied *immediately* after the behavior you wish to prevent, *every* time that behavior occurs"
(p. 357). Failure to be attentive to timing and consistency
will confuse the student, who may become tense, anxious,
and generally inhibited.

4. *Verbal warnings can be effective.* Dr. Funder (1997) describes how he conditioned his cat to stop scratching fur-
niture. "Whenever the cat started to claw the sofa, I made
a hissing sound and then immediately squirted the cat"
(p. 358). Soon he did not need the squirt bottle containing water; the hissing sound was sufficient to stop the behavior. With students, a verbal warning (not hissing)
might prove adequate.

5. *Don't send conflicting messages.* It's counterproductive to
send an "I'm sorry" message to a student soon after punishing him or her. If a punishment is deliberate and fair, you
should not experience guilt. Mixed messages are often motivated by guilt.

Dr. Funder also warns of five dangers of punishment:

1. Punishment arouses emotion in the teacher and the student.

2. It's difficult to be consistent in punishing because mood influences sensitivity to misbehavior as well as the punishment.

3. It's hard to gauge the severity of a punishment as experienced by the student.

4. Intended or not, punishment teaches that power prevails.

CHAPTER 3

5. Punishment is just as likely to motivate concealment as behavioral change.

THE VULNERABLE STUDENT

When you sign a contract to teach, protecting students from harm will not be a part of your job description. Nevertheless, creating a learning environment includes providing safety for all of your students. Students who feel physically or emotionally threatened are incapable of concentrating on academic work.

One researcher, Judith Bluestein, pursued an answer to the question, *Is the classroom an emotionally safe place?* She identified sixty-seven potential stressors for students in school environments (Bluestein 2001). Of course, some students are more vulnerable to physical and emotional harm than others. The psychological range of students is wide, running from fragile to very strong. Experience will enable you to recognize potential stressors and identify the students vulnerable to those stressors. It is especially important that you protect *targeted students*: those students singled out by other students for attack and ridicule.

Maintaining a safe environment for the vulnerable student will require vigilance. Whenever you see a student taunted or abused in any way, you must address it. Respond to the matter privately, since addressing an entire class or an individual in front of a class could add to the targeted student's problem. Two parties will require your attention: the mistreated student and the offending student(s). Clearly communicate to the mistreated students that they are deserving of respect and do not have to tolerate abuse. Also, sincerely communicate that you will work with them to develop nonviolent strategies for effectively responding to mistreatment. Your investment in helping them learn how to protect themselves will contribute to their confidence and self-sufficiency.

The offending students also will require your attention. Begin by giving them an opportunity to explain their behavior and then clearly communicate to them the inexcusability and unacceptability of predatory behavior. Further, while punishment is a possibility, emphasize character development. Abusing a fellow student is an act of weakness, not strength, not cowardice, not courage. Indicate that you are prepared to recruit their parents' participation in this work of character education.

Finally, in this post-Columbine world much research has been accomplished on the topic of bullying behavior. Avail yourself of the results of this work. The body of knowledge that exists to help you includes videos you might require bullying students to watch.

THE RESISTANT STUDENT

Just as there will be vulnerable students who will need protection, there will be resistant students who will make you feel the need to be protected. Resistant students will appear threatening because of their *odd* behavior. Mental health professionals have the diagnostic category ODD (oppositional defiant disorder).

ODD is a persistent pattern of negativistic, hostile, disobedient, and defiant behavior in a child or adolescent. Specific ODD behaviors include explosive anger, arguing with adults, denial of responsibility for one's own behavior, and using profanity. Two psychologists, Robert Brooks and Ross Greene, have addressed these behaviors. (Dr. Greene is the author of *The Explosive Child: A New Approach for Understanding and Parenting Easily Frustrated, Chronically Inflexible Children* [2000].) They offer advice regarding two strategic areas: orientation and conceptualization.

For *orientation*, there are six things to keep in mind that will maximize your effectiveness with resistant students. First, recognize that a problem is the difference between the ideal situation and reality, expressed as an equation: P = I-R. Ideally, every student will be pleasant and cooperative. In reality, you will encounter ODD behavior. Your challenge will be to reduce the problem since it's unlikely that you will be able to eliminate it. Second, working with angry and resistant students is part of the job. Do you still want the job? Remind yourself that the job has counterbalancing, positive features. Third, consider ways in which you might be contributing to the problem. Are you working too many hours? Is your lesson planning adequate? Are you getting seven to nine hours of sleep? Are unresolved personal problems eroding your patience?

Fourth, the one person whose behavior you can change is *you*. I suggest that you be selfish but in an enlightened way. Philosopher Ayn Rand defined selfishness as carefully considered self-interest (Rand 1961). Selfishly consider what you can do to make the problem more tolerable for you. This will make you more patient and understanding, which also will benefit the resistant student. When confronting a resistant student, ask questions that are authentic rather than rhetorical. For example, don't ask, "How many times do I have to tell you not to do that?" (Even if the student answers, "Twenty-three!" you haven't acquired useful information.) Instead, ask a question like "What you seem to be telling me is that you've decided not to do what I've asked. Is this what you're saying to me?"

Fifth, when interacting with resistant students, it's unrealistic to expect them to respond with a script you've written for them. Instead of insisting on word-for-word recitations, strive to get others to make and express decisions. Then respond to their declarations.

Sixth, there will be times when, in spite of your best and sincere effort, a resistant student will remain uncooperative. The parents of that student might tell you that this is evidence of your incompetence. Even worse, your principal might agree that your ineffectiveness is a reflection of your inability or inexperience. Don't believe them! Remember this: *Even God can't steer a parked car.* Ultimately students are responsible for their success or failure.

In addition to orientation, conceptualization of the problem will be helpful. Conceptualization means to consider something in terms of an idea or principle. Here are seven concepts that will help you construct an effective strategy for working with ODD students.

1. As challenging as it will be, make a deliberate effort to think and act in the student's best interest.
2. Research the student's history. Read what previous teachers have observed about the student.
3. Seek parental involvement. Like parents, you are an authority figure in the student's life. Ask the parents, "Am I describing a child who is familiar to you? Do you have any ideas or suggestions for me?"
4. Look for patterns in the student's ODD behavior. When does it occur? Where does it occur? With whom does it occur?
5. When punishing, respond to the ODD behavior. Don't react to the student's personality. (Remember Dr. Selzer's regrettable reaction to his uncooperative patient.)
6. Consider the possibility that a part of the student's day goes well. Seek out teachers with whom the student works cooperatively. Look for situations in which the student behaves desirably.

7. Look to the experts for help. Read what nationally recognized authorities, like Dr. Brooks and Dr. Greene, have written. Investigate the possibility that your school district or community has an expert on ODD.

The word *resist* is a verb meaning to take action to repel or impede an advancing force. Resistant students will perceive your approach as an invasion into their territory. Resistance might be a defensive action against the experience of failure. Resistance might be an expression of resentment against the imposition of authority. Never miss an opportunity to empathize with a student. If you can remember a time when you feared failure or resented an authority figure, you might recapture a time when you were resistant.

CHARACTER EDUCATION

Character education is closely related to discipline in that both are concerned with the development of personality traits. Harvard psychologist Gordon Allport went through an unabridged English dictionary and found 17,953 words describing human beings (Funder 1997). This tells us that (1) there are thousands of human characteristics, and (2) Gordon Allport needs a life. Character education is that part of teaching devoted to the nurturance of desirable qualities in students.

Of course, the inevitable question is, Whose desirable characteristics will be taught? The answer is, Everybody's. Certain qualities have been affirmed as desirable by all cultures and religions, regardless of when or where people have lived. *The Book of Virtue* by William Bennett (1993) lists these universal characteristics: self-discipline, responsibility, industriousness, courage, perseverance, honesty, loyalty, and compassion.

Consider the good effect on the learning environment when students are increasingly showing these qualities. Modeling these characteristics for your students will contribute to their character education and a favorable learning environment. Writer James Baldwin observes, "Children have never been very good at listening to their elders, but they have never failed to imitate them" (Kelly-Gangi and Patterson 2001).

4

WHAT IS MOTIVATION?

I never let school interfere with my education.

—Mark Twain

The Greek word *pneuma* can be translated as either *spirit* or *wind*. The Hebrew word *ruach* serves the same dual purpose. Both languages reflect the understanding that neither spirit nor wind can be seen and their presence is inferred from their effect. We never actually see the wind blowing but observe leaves in motion and weather vanes swinging. Like wind and spirit, motivation cannot be seen. Yet the starting point of every day of your professional life will be motivating your students to learn and yourself to teach.

Motivation is easy to define, difficult to understand, and challenging to incorporate. It's defined as *the ability to initiate and sustain goal-directed activity.* To appreciate the complexity of motivation, consider the everyday behavior of eating. The simplest explanation of our motivation to eat is hunger. However, a thorough understanding of why we eat includes physiological, sociocultural, and psychological considerations. Physiologically, the blood-sugar level signals the brain's hypothalamus that nourishment is needed. Socioculturally, we refer to certain parts of the day as *it's time to eat*. And some occasions are associated with not only eating but also certain kinds of food. Hungry or not, many spectators at a baseball game will eat a hot dog and moviegoers will eat popcorn. Further, some cultures feature food more than others. Italians are especially known for their love of food. Eating disorders demonstrate that the motivation to eat can be influenced by emotions. Often obesity is a result of the use of food as an antidepressant to the extreme of addiction. Anorexia nervosa can be driven by guilt or anxiety. An anorectic will not eat regardless of blood-sugar level, time of day, or occasion.

Psychology is the study of human behavior, and every introductory psychology textbook includes a chapter on motivation. Yet there is a sense in which all psychology is the study of motivation. Sigmund Freud, Abraham Maslow, and B. F. Skinner constructed different theories on motivation in their attempts to answer the question, Why do people behave as they do? My intention, or motivation, in the rest of this chapter is to provide you with helpful thoughts for motivating your students and yourself.

MOTIVATING STUDENTS TO LEARN

"All the desires, joys, and euphorias of a future life came rushing into me. Maybe this is how I handled the pain. I was so happy to be taking action" (Reilly 2003a). With these words twenty-seven-year-old Aron Ralston described how he saved his life by amputating his right arm with a dull pocketknife. Pinned by an eight-hundred-pound boulder for five days, Ralston concluded it was his only hope for survival. There is no mistaking Aron Ralston's motivation: he wanted to live.

"I've been coaching cross-country for 31 years and I've never met anyone with the drive Ben has. I don't think that there's an inch of that kid I haven't had to bandage up" (Reilly 2003b). With these words Hanna High School (Anderson, South Carolina) cross-country coach Chuck Parker describes Ben Comen. Ben has never finished higher than last in a cross-county meet. He covers the 3.1-mile course in a little less than an hour because of frequent falls followed by a lengthy, arduous getting up process. Ben Comen has cerebral palsy. His extraordinary motivation is not easily explained.

Motivating your students over 180 days of school will be a continual challenge. Accomplishing learning will not be a life-or-death matter, as with Aron Ralston. A remarkable person like Ben Comen is self-motivated and requires no help to stay on task. The humanistic psychologist Carl Rogers (1969) issues a challenge to teachers with these critical words:

> I become very irritated with the notion that students must be "motivated." The young human being is intrinsically motivated to a high degree. Many elements of his environment constitute challenges for him. He is curious, eager to discover, eager to know, eager to solve problems. A sad part of most education is that by the time the child has spent a number of years in school this intrinsic motivation is pretty well dampened. (p. 131)

The implicit good news in Rogers's observation is that by nature children are motivated to learn. Be encouraged that children are naturally curious and eager to discover, learn, and solve problems. This should make you optimistic about meeting the challenge to motivate. You'll be tapping into an existing desire rather than creating it.

When planning a teaching activity, address motivation by asking the following four questions:

1. Would I want to do this activity?
2. Why would my students want to do this activity?
3. Can I do my part of this lesson with enthusiasm?
4. Are my students capable of accomplishing what I'll be requiring of them?

A fifth question concerns intrinsic and extrinsic motivation. Intrinsic motivation is the drive from within to accomplish something. Intrinsically motivated people are moved by the satisfaction derived from accomplishment or the pleasure experienced in an activity. Extrinsically motivated people are moved by reward or avoidance of punishment. When planning, ask, Will my students be intrinsically or extrinsically motivated to do this work? If their motivation will be extrinsic, reward is more effective than punishment. Even so, there are critics of motivation by reward. Alfie Kohn (1993), the author of *Punished by Rewards*, has written that rewards are "likely to turn learning from an end to a means [and that] learning becomes something that must be gotten through in order to receive the reward" (p. 785). Rafi Esquith (2003) argues similarly in *There Are No Shortcuts* that the pleasure experienced when reading is sufficient motivation.

A stunning example of an intrinsically motivated reader is the late Eric Hoffer (1983). One of America's most noteworthy philosophers, he lost his eyesight at the age of seven in a fall down a flight of stairs. Eight years later Hoffer suddenly and inexplicably regained his sight. Fearing that he would again lose his ability to see, Hoffer decided to read as much as he could for as long as he could. He retained his sight for the rest of his life. Seven decades of reading eight or more hours a day eventually led to a professorship at Stanford University without having earned either a high school diploma or college degree. Like Mark Twain, he never allowed school to interfere with his education. Such was Hoffer's love of reading.

Granted, you could teach for fifty years without encountering a student as motivated as Eric Hoffer. To encourage you in motivating your students, here are four facts of life that have implications for motivation:

1. *Self-esteem comes from accomplishment.* There will be times when a spirited pep talk will help motivate students. However, your words will never do as much for students' self-esteem as their good performance. Pride and self-confidence are consequences of accomplishment.

2. *Explanatory style is important.* Francis Bacon writes, "Words twist and turn the understanding." How we account for our successes and failures significantly contributes to how we understand ourselves and others. Psychologists speak of internal and external controls. Students who hope you'll write an easy test believe their passing or failing depends on you. This would be an example of an external locus of control. Students with an internal locus of control take credit for passing and responsibility for failing. These students enjoy their success while students with an external locus of control will blame you for their failure.

3. *Relevance is an effective motivator.* It's almost impossible for a fifteen-year-old to appreciate the value of knowing the following math fact: the square of the hypotenuse equals the sum of the square of the other two sides. There is no substitute for relevancy in learning. Students are intrinsically motivated by the recognition of the usefulness of what they're learning. You'll not always be able to convince students of an immediate application to what they're learning. Nevertheless, strive to make the material relevant to their

lives. (An excellent example of a teacher incorporating relevance in instruction is the previously noted carpe diem scene in *Dead Poets Society*.)

4. *It's better to give up on someone too late than too soon.* In a criminal proceeding the accused is assumed innocent until proven guilty beyond a reasonable doubt. Similarly, assume students can be motivated until it's proven beyond a reasonable doubt that they can't be. Have an internal locus of control in your work by assuming that if you plan conscientiously, success will follow.

MOTIVATING YOURSELF TO TEACH

If you've not already heard this hackneyed saying, keep teaching and you will: *Those who can, do. Those who can't, teach. Those who can't teach, teach teachers.* However, Emily Moore (2000) has a different perspective. She is an English teacher. She's also a magna cum laude graduate of Princeton University. When asked why she wanted to be a teacher when she could have done anything, she responds,

> We live in an age when people seem to lament the state of public education in the same breath that they dismiss teachers as "those who can't." I cannot count the number of times a well-meaning acquaintance has assured me that I am qualified to do other things besides teach. That, by implication, I don't have to teach.
>
> In fact, I want to spend my life teaching. I love teaching. And ritzy degrees aside, I don't think I will ever feel qualified to do it as well as I'd like.
>
> I feel extraordinarily blessed to have been called to a profession in which I am always learning. It is grueling, exciting, gratifying work. (p. 13)

Emily believes she has been *called* to teaching, and her interests, talents, and skills correspond with her work. Further, she enjoys her work. A necessary part of motivating yourself to teach is the conviction that teaching is what you ought to be doing. With that conviction will come enjoyment and enthusiasm. Since you're going to be going to work for the next thirty-five years, isn't it a good idea to spend the day doing something you enjoy? Many people work at something they don't enjoy. They are extrinsically motivated by meeting financial responsibilities. That is a commendable motivation. However, it will be an advantage to you throughout your career if you feel blessed to be a teacher.

Students can tell which teachers enjoy their work. If you doubt this, then think about your own teachers. Didn't some leave you with the impression they enjoyed being teachers? Weren't there others who seemed to be ROAD (retired on active duty)? Two things to keep in mind that will help you retain energy and enthusiasm for your work are concerned with purpose and burnout.

The assurance that as a teacher you are making a difference is one of the things that will motivate you in the years ahead. Knowing that you are influencing the lives of your students and others will give purpose to your work. Unfortunately, teachers are susceptible to the George Bailey syndrome. If you've seen the movie classic *It's a Wonderful Life*, you're familiar with this syndrome. Convinced that his life has counted for nothing, George Bailey cries out, "I wish I'd never been born!" Through angelic intervention George is given a vision of what the lives of numerous people would've been like if he'd never been born. The differences are striking.

Like George Bailey, you'll occasionally feel that your labor is in vain. Don't count on having an angel to convince you otherwise. Instead, draw reassurance from students and parents who have told you that they're fortunate you chose to be a teacher.

Burned-out teachers have lost energy, enthusiasm, and a sense of purpose for their work. These losses occur gradually and often imperceptibly. Burnout among professionals has been the topic of innumerable books, in-service days, and workshops. Many more than the following four suggestions are available to teachers seeking to be proactive about burnout:

1. *Be aware that it can happen to you.* In the early years of teaching, burnout seems like something that happens to other teachers. You'll see older teachers lacking vitality and marvel that their condition exists. But it can happen to you. Don't assume that your love of teaching provides immunity from burnout. An unguarded strength is a double weakness. A saying among boxers is that it's the punch you don't see coming that knocks you down.

2. *Be student-centered.* There's a world of difference between teaching twenty years and teaching one year twenty times. In addition to annually revising your lesson plans, be student-centered. Draw energy from your students' excitement. Be mindful that material that is old for you is new for them. Several years ago I heard a veteran funeral director speaking to students in training to be funeral directors. To them he said, "I've arranged thousands of funerals, but the next one I do will be my first. Why? Because it will be the first one I will arrange for this person and this family."

3. *Plan lessons that include things you'll enjoy.* One of my most pleasant surprises as a teacher has been genuinely enjoying parts of lessons I've presented dozens of times. There are poems, stories, simulations, games, and video excerpts I've experienced countless times and still look forward to them. You will not earn extra credit or an award for trudging through lessons you find barely tolerable.

4. *Seek out new ideas.* In addition to conversations with your colleagues, ideas for doing the same things differently can come from conferences, workshops, in-service days, and reading. If you're not satisfied with a lesson, change it. Mental health professionals have informally defined insanity as *repeating the same behavior expecting a different result.* If something's not worked twice, why would anyone expect it to work the third time without modification? Often courage is required for change. If you find yourself fearful or even tentative about change, consider these words from the movie *The Princess Diaries* (2001):

> Courage is not the absence of fear, but rather the judgment that something else is more important than fear. The brave may not live forever, but the cautious do not live at all. From now on you will be traveling the road between who you think you are and who you can be. The key is to allow yourself to make the journey.

Finally, as important as your work will be, it can't be all of your life. You must have a life apart from teaching. In a presentation on leadership, General Colin Powell (2002) stated,

> Have fun in your command. Don't always run at breakneck pace. Take leave when you've earned it. Spend time with your families. Corollary: Surround yourself with people who take their work seriously, but not themselves, those who work hard and play hard.

5

WHAT DOES IT MEAN TO BE INTELLIGENT?

You have to be careful if you're good at something, to make sure you don't think you're good at other things that you aren't necessarily so good at. . . . Because I've been very successful at [software development] people come in and expect that I have wisdom about topics that I don't.

—Bill Gates

The I.Q. test was invented to predict academic performance, nothing else. If we wanted something that would predict life success, we'd have to invent another test completely.

—Robert Zajonc

Aoccdrnig to rscheearch at Cmabrigde Uinervtisy, it deosn't mttaer waht oredr the ltteers in a wrod are, the olny iprmoetnt tihng is taht the frist and lsat ltteer be at the rghit pclae. The rset can be a taotl mses and you can sitll raed it wouthit a porbelm. Tihs is bcuseae the huamn mnid deos not raed ervey lteter by istlef, but the wrod as a wlohe.

How did you do reading the previous paragraph? Are you surprised that you were able to make sense of it so easily? Intelligence is the ability to learn from experience, solve problems, and use knowledge to adapt to new situations. Your ability to reconfigure the letters of the misspelled words and make sense of that paragraph is a demonstration of your intelligence. Every day you acquire information that you store for retrieval. Retrieval occurs when you draw on that information to solve a problem or adapt to a situation.

How effective is your ability to store and retrieve information? It's effective enough for you to answer the following question: What do the following ten quotations have in common?

1. "Go ahead, make my day."
2. "I see dead people."
3. "If you build it he will come."
4. "The truth? The truth? You can't handle the truth!"
5. "Houston, we have a problem."
6. "Hasta la vista, baby."
7. "Toto, I don't think we're in Kansas."
8. "I have the need, the need for speed."
9. "Are you talking to me?"
10. "I'm going to make him an offer he can't refuse."

Even if you aren't familiar with all ten of these quotations, you probably recognized enough of them to conclude that all of them come from movies. In so doing, not only did you retrieve knowledge but you analyzed enough of the quotations to synthesize a conclusion. *Knowledge, analysis,* and *synthesis* are words you recognize from Bloom's taxonomy, described in the second chapter. Part of the work of teaching is to nurture your students' intelligence by utilizing the full range of mental processing: knowledge, comprehension, analysis, application, synthesis, and evaluation.

Effective teachers also see intelligence as something that can be expressed as any one of several abilities, such as doing well in school, managing everyday tasks, or creating novel ideas. An even more diverse view of intelligence is Howard Gardner's theory of multiple intelligences in which he describes at least seven intelligences (Gardner 1983, 1999). Dr. Gardner's theory is summarized in Table 5.1.

Gardner's work as an educational psychologist began as a boy when he was attracted to reading biographies. Later, when studying intelligence, he noted that many famous people were not intelligent in the traditional, math–verbal sense. From that realization he concluded there are other ways in which people demonstrate the ability to acquire and utilize knowledge. The implication and application of Gardner's work for all teachers is that they be receptive to the variety of ways in which students can be viewed and encouraged as intelligent.

At the beginning of this chapter you read a sentence consisting of words with incorrectly placed letters. Perhaps you were

Table 5.1. A Summary of Howard Gardner's Theory of Multiple Intelligences

Intelligence	Characteristic	Who Has It?
Verbal-linguistic	Use words effectively	William Shakespeare (Playwright and poet)
Logical-mathematical	Recognize numerical patterns and present ideas in a logical sequence	Albert Einstein (Physicist)
Spatial	Judge distance and visualize objects in motion	Bobby Fischer (Chess champion)
Kinesthetic	Sense one's own body in motion; coordinated	Tiger Woods (Professional golfer)
Musical	Discern pitch and rhythm and create musical pieces	Ludwig van Beethoven (Composer)
Interpersonal	Sense what others are feeling and relate to them	Sigmund Freud (Psychiatrist)
Intrapersonal	Identify, understand, and manage one's emotional life	Dalai Lama (Buddhism's spiritual leader)

surprised by how easily you corrected the misspellings and made sense of the sentence. Human intelligence is a fascinating phenomenon. In the years ahead, if you study your students to understand how they acquire, store, retrieve, and utilize information, you will never lack for wonder.

If you need more evidence that intelligence is a wonder, consider the savant syndrome. People affected by this syndrome, many of whom are autistic, have islands of brilliance existing in the absence of language ability. Expressions of this syndrome include the ability to perform incredible mathematical computations, musical pieces, and feats of memory. Kim Peek, the inspiration for the character Raymond in the movie *Rain Man*, has memorized over seventy-five hundred books in addition to all the area and zip codes in the United States. Yet he depends on his father to manage the ordinary tasks of daily life. Howard Gardner is not without his critics. However, everyone who has studied intelligence agrees that it is a source of wonder.

FOUR INSTRUCTIONAL STRATEGIES

Do you consider yourself an intelligent person? Answering that question yes or no demonstrates that you have in mind a definition and understanding of intelligence. If the word *intelligent* had no meaning for you, then you would be unable to answer the question.

You don't have to be familiar with the theory of multiple intelligences, know the dictionary definition of intelligent, or have the results of your IQ test in order to know if you're intelligent. Like most people, you have a sense of your intelligence from your history. Your perception of your intelligence has developed from grades and evaluations provided by teachers and comments from other people in your life. Also, through the years you've developed a self-concept of your capability of learning new material and solving problems.

Intelligence is a concept that has practical application for teachers, since the ultimate goal of teaching is student understanding. Students demonstrate understanding; then they take knowledge, skills, and concepts and apply them in problem solving. Also, understanding is shown when judgments (critical analysis) are made. In a single word, a necessary goal of teaching is to get students to *think*. Approximately one hundred years ago Ivan Pavlov conditioned a dog to salivate at the sound of a tuning fork. In what is perhaps psychology's most famous experiment Pavlov did not teach a dog to think. With neither deliberation nor understanding the dog reacted to a stimulus. Teaching is not a Pavlovian endeavor.

Terminology comes and goes, but the ideas behind the jargon are constant. The following strategies for nurturing students' thinking and problem-solving abilities are the current vogue in nomenclature. *Constructivism, discovery learning, level of processing theory,* and *self-regulation* are instructional strategies that have been used by effective teachers for centuries. As you read the brief descriptions of these four strategies, don't be surprised if you recognize them as approaches used by effective teachers you've had.

Constructivism emphasizes the active role of the student in building an understanding of information provided by the teacher. An example of this approach is the use of document-based questions (DBQs) in which a student is given a primary source like Lincoln's Gettysburg Address and asked to construct a description of Lincoln's political philosophy. Constructivism requires the teacher to ask divergent rather than convergent questions. Divergent questions encourage analysis and interpretation because they do not have a single correct answer. In the example above, a convergent question would be "In what year was this speech given?" A divergent question would be "Why is this speech one of the most famous speeches in American history?"

Discovery learning emphasizes the formulation and testing of a hypothesis. Perhaps you recognize this as the scientific method introduced in your first science laboratory exercise. The sequence of investigation in discovery learning is observation, hypothesis, experimentation, and conclusion. Discovery learning requires making a statement that something is believed to be true and devising a procedure for verifying or falsifying that statement.

Level of processing theory emphasizes that a student's ability to recall information is related to how deeply it has been processed and related to other information. Crucial to this strategy is *wait time*, which requires the teacher to allow time for students to struggle. An example of this strategy would be giving students a Shakespearean quotation and sufficient time to analyze its meaning and describe how it might apply it to their own lives. (Perhaps you've recognized the relationship between level of processing theory and constructivism.)

Self-regulation is a teaching/learning process in which students exercise choices within a framework structured by the teacher. The intended result of this strategy is a discovery learning experience. An example of choice within a framework would be a written book report on any autobiography (choice); the report must be typed, double-spaced, 750–1250 words, and include information about the person's family, childhood, education, and religion (framework). An important feature of self-regulation in particular and teaching in general is that students experience freedom when making choices. However, it is equally important that students not experience anxiety, frustration, and fear of failure from uncertainty in regard to your expectations.

CHALLENGING A STUDENT'S ASSUMPTIVE WORLD

The brilliant and controversial psychiatrist Thomas Szasz (1973) writes,

> Every act of conscious learning requires the willingness to suffer an injury to one's self-esteem. That is why young children, before they are aware of their own self-importance, learn so easily, and why older persons, especially if vain or important, cannot learn at all. (p. 18)

When someone's assumptive world is challenged, a belief held by that person is being called into question. If it is a long-standing belief held with intensity, the individual is likely to resist yielding it. Dr. Szasz believes that changing our minds, which is one way of learning, becomes more difficult with age.

Educational psychologists have several terms for challenging the assumptive world: *belief persistence, cognitive dissonance,* and *upsetting a stable context.* All refer to an experience that suggests a change of mind is in order. Ernest Thayer's classic poem, "Casey at the Bat," is an example of such an experience. It describes a baseball game in which the home-team fans, certain that their hero will deliver the game-winning hit, watch incredulously as he strikes out. The last line of the poem is "There is no joy in Mudville/Mighty Casey has struck out." The fans' unquestioned belief that Casey would never let them down is challenged by experience.

In his inspiring and moving memoir, journalist Richard Cohen (2004) describes the experience of being ravaged by multiple sclerosis, blindness, and cancer. The physically compromised state of his body compels him to abandon his former belief of what it means to be a man.

I feel weak because I acknowledge the realities of my life. We exist in a culture that celebrates strength. Men are strong and self-reliant. I am weakened and need the help of others. There is no escape from the rust I see on my body.

I must rise above the culture of perfection and remember that I can *be* even if I can no longer *do*. I am learning to acknowledge weakness, accept assistance, and discover new forms of self-definition. My formula has changed. I do not read self-absorbed men's magazines or go to Vin Diesel movies. A new male ideal will have to do and might even save me. I will just have to create it. I cannot allow myself to be held captive by old dreams. (pp. 222–23)

Richard Cohen is learning by overcoming belief persistence. By changing his mind about manhood and redefining it, he is living above self-pity and engaging in the joys that are available to him.

6

WHAT DOES EVERY TEACHER NEED TO KNOW ABOUT LESSON PLANNING?

Education is not the filling of a pail, but the lighting of a fire.

—William Butler Yeats

Always in our presentation we must give something which does not exceed the child's powers, and yet at the same time calls forth effort.

—Maria Montessori

While I'm not a big fan of bumper sticker philosophy, I do appreciate these mottos:

- A failure to plan is a plan to fail.
- Plan your work and work your plan.

You can have all the enthusiasm in the world, but without a carefully considered plan you will be more of an entertainer than a teacher. Passion will never substitute for preparation. It will never compensate for a lack of planning.

THE FOUR-PART LESSON PLAN

Colin Powell (2002) has said that "great leaders are almost always great simplifiers" (p. 124). The same is true of teachers. (Aren't teachers leaders?) There are many variations on the theme of lesson planning. For all the differences among lesson-planning formats, four elements are present in all of them: introduction, objectives, methodology, and evaluation.

Speeches, sermons, lectures, and other informative presentations share the general format of *tell what you're going to say, say it,* and *review what you've said.* This three-part approach also applies to lessons. Your introduction provides students with a preview of the lesson and why the material is worth knowing. The methodology is the means by which the material will be communicated and reinforced. The evaluation will inform you of whether or not your objectives have been accomplished.

A helpful sequence for structuring the introductory part of your lesson is topic, problem, and rationale. For example, "We are going to study Robert Frost's poem 'The Road Not Taken' to understand its message so that we can be better prepared to make decisions." The topic, problem, and rationale sequence is used in research and takes the form of "We are going to study *x* in order to understand *y* so that *z*."

Objectives, also referred to as learning outcomes, must be stated in terms of the student. Statements of objectives begin with the words, *the student will be able to,* not *I am going to.* An objective cannot be "I am going to spend twenty minutes showing a video excerpt." Although that goal could be evaluated by looking at the clock, it would tell you nothing about student accomplishments. In anticipation of the *evaluation* part of your lesson you should add the word *demonstrate* to the phrase *the student will be able to.* That will help you structure the evaluation because it will tell you what you expect your students to show you. Going back to the example of the Frost poem, one objective could be *The student will be able to demonstrate a knowledge and understanding of this poem by writing a 250–300 word essay paraphrasing the poem.*

Methodology describes how you intend to accomplish what you envision accomplishing. This part of your lesson requires a realistic estimate of the time each activity will take. Do not be overly optimistic about student participation. Allotting twenty minutes for discussion doesn't mean that's what you're going to get. Be prepared to lecture or make some other presentation to accomplish what you hope to do by discussion.

Finally, given approximately fifty minutes of class time, strive to use more than one mode of instruction. For example, begin with a fifteen- to twenty-minute introductory lecture followed by a ten-minute video excerpt, and conclude with a twenty-minute discussion. Have a twenty-minute writing assignment or evaluative quiz prepared in case the discussion doesn't develop. Be mindful that discussions are better encouraged by *divergent* rather than *convergent* questions. The former are open-ended, inviting many answers. The latter stifle discussion by calling for a single answer, usually a fact. "Do you agree with Frost's analysis of decision making?" is a *divergent* question. "Who wrote the poem 'The Road Not Taken?'" is a *convergent* question.

Evaluation is guided by your stated objectives. When preparing the last part of your lesson plan, ask yourself, "What do I want to measure?" The answer will be provided by your stated intentions for your students. To refer again to Bloom's taxonomy, if your objectives include comprehension, analysis, and application then your evaluation must test in those areas.

In his twenty-two seasons as a major league baseball player, Babe Ruth struck out 1,330 times (a record). In a full season he went to bat approximately six hundred times. Therefore, it could be said that Babe Ruth had two years in which he did nothing but strike out. In spite of two full seasons of statistical failure, Babe

Ruth has an honored place in the Baseball Hall of Fame because he also set home run records that stood for decades.

In teaching, as well as baseball, poor performances are inevitable. Creative reflection is the practice of constructively examining why a lesson failed and what can be tried to prevent similar failures in the future. Creative reflection is the teacher's autopsy, performed to determine a lesson's cause of death. How a disappointing lesson is examined and understood will determine if its failure will be repeated. The following are six suggestions for reconsidering a lesson that largely failed (Malikow 2005).

First, don't overreact to a disappointing lesson by overgeneralizing about yourself as a teacher. Global statements like "I'm a total failure" and "I can't do anything right" are neither helpful nor accurate. If you were completely incompetent, you would have been weeded out during your teacher education program. You accomplished your degree and were hired because you've demonstrated competency and promise as a teacher. Don't overreact with self-flagellation, born of guilt. Guilt is a temporary condition; it is a tool to be used and then put away.

Second, get some emotional and temporal distance from the failed lesson and then carefully review your lesson plan. A day or two after the lesson, reconsider your plan's introduction, objectives, methodology, and evaluation. Don't overgeneralize about the lesson plan. Be specific about what did and didn't work well. Separate the parts that went well from those that didn't and try to acquire an understanding of when and why certain parts failed.

Third, have an internal locus of control in your analysis. Be fully responsible for the factors that were in your control and will be in your control in the future. Consider such things as the time and effort you put into the lesson and the enthusiasm you had for the material. Ask yourself questions relevant to your sphere of influence. Did I get enough sleep the night before? Was I preoccupied by something the day of the lesson? Was I confident that I was well-prepared? Was I convinced of the value of this material for my students?

Fourth, rarely will a lesson's failure be entirely your fault. Account for factors that contributed to the disappointment. Were there any conditions that might have distracted or excited your students, like a fight in the cafeteria, a heavy snowfall suggesting an early school dismissal, or an after-school athletic event? Consider the time and day of the lesson. (Is there any time more challenging for maintaining students' attention that the last period on Friday?) Reflect on how class went the day before the failed lesson. The previous day is part of the following day's orientation. Finally, remind yourself that there are students who are determined not to cooperate and are committed to disrupting your best effort.

Fifth, after you've taken counsel with yourself, debrief with a senior faculty member or teacher mentor. Describe the lesson without analysis, giving your colleague an opportunity to provide an uninfluenced interpretation. Prepare specific questions for the meeting and expect to be asked questions. Resist the impulse to defend yourself; this meeting is part of your continuing education, not a trial.

Sixth, consider doing research. Any problem you experience also confronts other teachers. Every problem encountered by teachers has been the subject of research. Investigate what the experts have to offer. A problem not faced is a problem not solved. Even if an immediate and complete solution is not available, the process of improving things can begin. Shakespeare wrote, "How poor are they that have not patience! What wound did ever heal but by degrees?" (*Othello* 2.3.371).

Resiliency is an object's ability to return to its original form. Rubber bands are resilient. Another way of considering resiliency is the ability to bounce back. Drop a bowling ball and you'll see that it is not resilient. In contrast, a superball is remarkably resilient, bouncing far above the point from which it was released. Creative reflection can result in a teacher bouncing back from a failed lesson to a place of even higher competence.

For Babe Ruth, one time at bat was part of a game, a game was part of a season, and a season was part of a career. To consider only his strikeouts would be a distortion of a great career. For a teacher, a lesson is a part of a day; a day is a part of a school year; and a school year is a part of a career.

TEACHING IN THE AFFECTIVE DOMAIN

Have you ever read a book because it was assigned and then read all the books written by that author? Have you ever taken a course because it was required and then considered changing your major? Have you ever tried something like Thai food or learned to play something like tennis and then it became part of your life? If so, then you've had an affective domain experience.

Psychologists speak of cognitive (or knowing) and affective (or feeling) experiences. Learning is an intellectual exercise. That's an obvious statement that doesn't need defending. Less obvious is that learning is an affective experience. Students who say, "I love Shakespeare" or "I hate geometry," are reporting what they feel.

Dare to believe that you can teach with such creativity and enthusiasm that students will come to love what you love. Does this seem unrealistic and perfectionistic to you? If so, consider the words of legendary football coach Vince Lombardi: "If you chase perfection, you will catch excellence." Aim for more than you are likely to attain. The implication of Lombardi's philosophy is that if you pursue excellence, you will catch mediocrity, and if you chase mediocrity you'll catch failure.

Table 6.1. The Five-Stage Progression of Teaching in the Affective Domain

Verb	Noun	Example
1. Receiving	Compliance	Doing weight training as a required part of a required course
2. Responding	Enjoyment	Realizing that for the first time you're looking forward to physical education class
3. Valuing	Importance	Commenting to a friend that you're surprised at how good it feels to weight train
4. Organizing	Arrangement	Continuing to exercise with weights *after* the class weight-training unit ends
5. Integrating	Commitment	Buying a membership to a health club and hiring a personal trainer

In your lesson planning consider how you can make your passion infectious. Of course, you can't give what you don't have. And you won't have passion for everything you teach. But when you recognize a love for something, consider why you feel as you do and how this attitude can be nurtured in your students.

Table 6.1 shows the five-stage progression of teaching in the affective domain.

A mind-set that might help you in the challenge of teaching in the affective domain is that of Mary Pipher. In her best seller *Reviving Ophelia*, Dr. Pipher (1994) describes her attitude toward her work as an adolescent therapist. Her goals for her clients, while ambitious, are adaptable to the work of teaching.

My general goals for all clients are to increase their authenticity, openness to experience, competence, flexible thinking, and realistic appraisal of their environment. I want to help clients see things in new ways and develop richer, more rewarding relationships. (p. 250)

7

HOW DO I DETERMINE GRADES?

[If] bonuses for high scores are dangled in front of teachers or schools—or punitive "consequences" are threatened for low scores—the chances are far greater that a meaningful curriculum will be elbowed out to make room for test-oriented instruction.

—Alfie Kohn

A few years ago a graduate student at Le Moyne College wrote a master's thesis presenting the results of his research on misperceptions of teaching. Although he had taught only a couple of years, he sensed that people outside of the profession have an inaccurate picture of a teacher's work. One common misperception he found concerned working hours. According to his study, nonteachers believe teachers work a traditional eight-hour day and forty-hour week. One reason teachers exceed those hours is the time they give to writing and correcting tests and other assignments.

In addition to being time-consuming, this work is often tedious and sometimes disheartening. Assigning grades will be an emotionally charged interaction between you and your students. Reflect on how it felt when you received a grade other than the one you expected. An empathic experience for you will be when your principal observes and evaluates your work.

GRADING, MOTIVATING, AND RELATING TO STUDENTS

You might be tempted to not write your own tests. Textbook publishers and well-meaning colleagues will offer you tests they've produced. When you're pressed for time, the temptation to use somebody else's test will be strong. I urge you to resist it. Only you will know what you've covered, especially the material you've emphasized. Nobody knows better than you the methodologies and vocabulary of the instruction you provided. Don't put yourself in the uncomfortable position of defending somebody else's test.

As already noted, grade assignment is an emotionally charged part of a teacher–student relationship. It's imperative that not every communication between a teacher and student be tied to a grade. When the communication involves a grade, be aware that the difference between a B minus and C plus could be slight for you but a quality-of-life issue for a C student. Give students an opportunity to make a case for a higher grade and explain why it's important. (Of course, if the opportunity would not be authentic, don't give it. Don't make believe you're receptive to a proposal when you're not.)

Guard against the halo effect, in which knowing the identity of the student whose work you're evaluating influences the grade. Granted, as the year continues you'll come to recognize a student's writing style and handwriting. When that happens, as an act of self-discipline and professionalism, remind yourself that an A student must earn every A and a D student deserves a chance.

Grades are extrinsic motivators. However, when the material being tested is meaningful to the student, the testing experience has an intrinsic component. Make an effort to ask questions that call for a practical application of the material. Bear in mind that intelligence is the ability to acquire and utilize knowledge in the work of problem solving.

TYPES OF TESTS

Although you may not be an expert on test production, you have a lot of experience in test consumption. Since you've taken hundreds of tests through the years, testing and evaluation is another area of teaching in which your experience as a student will be an asset.

In a sense there are only two types of tests, good and bad, and from experience you know the characteristics of each. Your students might tell you that a good test is one that is fair. Further, they might define a fair test as one that is easy to pass. At first, that definition of fair sounds laughable. However, on closer examination, it can be quite informative.

While a fair test may not be easy to pass, it's easier to pass than an unfair one. Fair (or good) tests have no surprises for the students. Fair tests reflect the material that has been emphasized in class (instruction) and out of class (assignments).

Fair tests have no trick questions. There's a story of the teacher whose true-false quiz began with the written directions: *If the correct answer is true, write false. If the correct answer is false, write true.* Of course, the students who knew the material but didn't read the directions did poorly on the quiz. That's an amusing story and the teacher cleverly made a point about reading directions. However, students who didn't know the material and neglected to read the directions probably achieved the highest grades. That's hardly fair. Neither was it amusing to the students who did poorly.

In a fair test, the only reason for students to miss a question is that they don't know the requisite material. In a fair test a student will not miss a question because of the question itself. It can be demoralizing for a student to know the material but not be able to demonstrate it because of a poorly constructed question. Test construction involves writing, and all writing requires repeated proofreading. Have at least one other knowledgeable person read your test. You're likely to find yourself embarrassed if the first proofreading is when your students take the test. Still worse, your embarrassment could result in misdirected anger toward your students. (Psychologists refer to this as blaming the victims.)

Clarity is important in the wording of questions. It's also important in communicating criteria for evaluation. Have you ever read an essay question and asked yourself, *What is this teacher looking for?* If so, possibly you were uncertain of the essay's required length, content, and degree of detail. Taking a test is work and every job has its specifications. Students need specifications.

Fair tests can be completed by a conscientious student in the time provided. You will never write a test that is completed by all students in same amount of time. Unless completing the test within a specified time is part of what you're testing, each student should have as much time as needed to complete the test. Again, it can be demoralizing for a student to know the material but not be able to demonstrate it.

There is another way of considering types of tests that is related to fairness. There are at least five formats for tests (see Table 7.1). The format you choose should depend on the skill you are seeking to evaluate.

Table 7.1. **Five Types of Tests**

Format	Skill
1. Multiple-choice questions	Recognize
2. Project assignment	Construct
3. Practical examination	Perform
4. Portfolio evaluation	Create
5. Essay evaluation	Write

Writing multiple-choice questions that are not multiple-guess is a challenge. As in all writing, this will require time. The time consumed by carefully constructing multiple-choice tests is regained by their quick correction. Also referred to as objective tests, they have the misleading reputation of being able to measure only fact acquisition. Thoughtfully constructed multiple-choice questions can evaluate students' abilities in comprehension, application, analysis, synthesis, and assessment.

The *stem* of a multiple-choice question asks the question or poses the problem. *Options* are the alternatives for answering or responding. Incorrect options are *foils*, sometimes referred to as *distractors*. Here are eight guidelines for writing effective, student-friendly objective questions:

1. The stem should ask a single question or pose one problem.
2. Include as much wording as possible in the stem.
3. Strive to limit the options to no more than two words.
4. Avoid negative language in favor of positive wording that uses fewer words and is easier to understand. (The previous sentence rewritten using negative language would look like this: Do not use negative language. Instead, use positive wording that doesn't use as many words and isn't as difficult to understand.)
5. Make it easier for students to consider options by placing them vertically instead of horizontally.

6. Check the answers for patterns, like the tendencies for "C" or "True" as the correct responses.
7. Have someone proofread your test for compositional errors, ambiguities, and grammatical hints of correct answers.
8. Do not give information in one part of your test that provides the correct answer in another part.

Each format requires students to demonstrate a different skill. Multiple-choice questions challenge students to recognize correct answers. Project assignments call for students to construct something. (Did you ever make a science project for a science fair? If so, you've experienced a project assignment.) A portfolio assessment is a collection of works in which a student shows creativity. If you have a driver's license, you've taken a practical test in which you demonstrated competency by performance.

A venue for evaluation loved by some students and feared by others is the essay test. Of course, an essay is a demonstration of writing ability. Essay questions can be written to require a student to display and apply knowledge, show understanding, analyze, create, and make judgments. In an essay a student expresses the process by which a conclusion was reached. Teachers who assign essays, like math teachers, are requiring students to show their work.

Essay questions can appear in a variety of forms and provide a means for evaluating different skills. An essay assignment popular among social studies teachers is *document-based questions*. Also referred to as DBQs, they provide students with a body of information and then ask questions related to that data. For example, students are given a copy of the Declaration of Independence or Martin Luther King's *Letter from a Birmingham Jail* and are asked questions about the American Revolution or civil rights movement. Another form of essay question is the *reflection paper*.

Students are required to describe an experience and express related thoughts and feelings. For example, students are asked to describe and reflect on September 11, 2001, or their proudest accomplishment.

In reading this section, you may have noted overlap. The skill measured by one type of test can also be evaluated by other types of tests. A portfolio examination assesses creativity, which also can be evaluated through an essay. Responding to essay questions can call for analytical ability, but multiple-choice questions also can require analysis. When preparing a test, ask yourself, What am I seeking to measure? What are my objectives as stated in my lesson plans? What is the best testing instrument for evaluating success in accomplishing those objectives? In summary, be able to defend any test you give.

VALIDITY AND RELIABILITY

Every spring, professional football scouts test hundreds of college football players in anticipation of the annual National Football League draft, when teams select college players. Predicting who these players are requires *valid* and *reliable* testing.

A test is valid if it measures what it claims to measure. A test is reliable if it produces similar results regardless of who evaluates it. Further, reliable tests are unaffected by when and where they are given.

Football scouts have tests for evaluating prospective players' speed, strength, and agility. A player who runs a forty-yard dash in 4.2 seconds is unquestionably fast. A prospect who bench presses 225 pounds for thirty-five repetitions is undisputedly strong. These tests are valid because they measure the abilities they claim to measure. Also, they depend entirely on the athlete. The results are uninfluenced by the time of day or place of testing.

Neither are the results affected by which scout is holding the stopwatch or counting the repetitions.

For predictive testing, validity and reliability are necessary but not sufficient. Other tests are involved in evaluating these athletes. Forecasting performance as a professional football player is like predicting success as a college student. The SAT (Scholastic Aptitude Test) is valid as a measurement of mathematical and verbal abilities. Also, the SAT is reliable as described above. Nobody would deny that mathematical and verbal abilities are assets for college students. However, like speed and strength for football players, mathematical and verbal abilities are only two of the indicators of future success in college.

There are undergraduate and graduate education courses devoted entirely to tests and measurement. You have probably already taken one. Regardless of the extent of your formal training in constructing tests and evaluating results, remember the words *valid* and *reliable*.

Remember the Vince Lombardi quotation about pursuing perfection? ("If you chase perfection, you will catch excellence.") The perfect test measures what it claims to measure and only what it claims to measure. The results of the perfect test are unaffected by when and where it was given and who evaluates it. The perfect test is the test you'll never write but should always try to write.

THE WORK OF CORRECTION

Did you know that . . . ?

- Socrates died from an overdose of wedlock.
- Sir Francis Drake circumcised the world with a hundred-foot clipper.

- John Milton wrote *Paradise Lost*. Then his wife died and he wrote *Paradise Regained*.
- Abraham Lincoln was born in a log cabin, which he built with his own hands.
- The famous composer Handel was half German, half Italian, and half English.
- Cyrus McCormick invented the raper, which did the work of a hundred men.

All of the above bloopers are excerpts from essays written by students (Lederer 2005, pp. 23–28). Herm Card (1998), an English teacher and poet, describes the work of correction in *Between the Lines*.

BETWEEN THE LINES

All that prevents him from
devoting his total attention
to the baseball game
is the pile of student writing
between him and the TV,
a stack of cliches and
tired metaphors,
worn out by a thousand previous users,
and abusers,
of the language.

He sifts through the pile
looking for one which will
motivate him to continue on
to a second and a third,
and so forth,
a metaphorical rounding of the bases,

until he has reduced the pile to nothing,
and able to turn his full attention to
the Yankees and Red Sox.

Glancing above his glasses to catch the replay
of Derek Jeter rocking a line drive
off the green monster
and only getting a single,
he ponders the mysterious twist of baseball fate
that penalizes a player for hitting the ball
too hard,
like he is penalizing himself for caring
too much,
about grading these papers.

So he pores over them
with the Fenway crowd noise
as background
until he chances across a phrase
which makes him grab the remote
and click the ball game into darkness
and stare at the screen
to see the image which has leapt off
the page in front of him
far more vivid than the night-game-green
of Fenway's infield,
reverberating louder than
the crack of Derek's bat. (p. 48)

It isn't always a student's unintended humor that will provide a break from the ennui of essay correcting. Sometimes relief will come from a stunning phrase or arresting bit of insight.

The hours teacher spend reading and correcting students' work is largely unappreciated labor. Students and parents aren't aware of the time required for a careful reading and correcting of written work. Further, since people rarely enjoy being corrected, some students will resent you for your effort.

The work of correction is a service you provide as a professional. It is something you contribute to your students' development as learners. It is a part of your job that requires expertise, conscientiousness, self-discipline, and, of course, time. It might also require anger management if you see a student roll into a ball and toss in the wastebasket a paper you spent twenty minutes correcting.

Aristotle said, "We cannot learn without pain," (p. 46) and Helen Keller spoke of "the flush of victory and the heart-sinking of disappointment" (p. 24) as necessary educational experiences (Kelly-Gangi and Patterson 2001). I trust you will never intentionally visit pain and disappointment on a student. You can encourage students by strategically mingling authentic affirmation with corrective comments. The work of correction should include observations that will give students that flush of victory. This is a part of teaching that will be enriched by empathy. Never lose the feeling of what it was like to have your own work scrutinized and evaluated.

8

IS THERE ANYTHING ELSE I NEED TO KNOW?

One looks back with appreciation to the brilliant teachers, but with gratitude to those who touched our human feelings. The curriculum is so much necessary raw material, but warmth is the vital element for the growing plant and for the soul of a child.

—Carl Jung

You might not be able to do things like a person who can see. But there are always two ways to do everything. You've just got to find the other way.

—Ray Charles's mother

Carl Jung's words express something every teacher needs to know: students don't care how much you know until they know how much you care. There is no sentiment that will adequately substitute for genuinely caring about your students' development as human beings. This genuine care is both taught and caught. Your decision to be a teacher suggests that you have been exposed to people who cared about you and you've incurred this good infection. Be encouraged in your work by reminding yourself that you're a teacher because you found teaching *and* teaching found you.

Teaching calls for resiliency and creativity. The words of Ray Charles's mother provide advice for all of us who teach. We might not be able to do things like other teachers who have abilities we lack. But we can bounce back from the disappointment of not having gifts we admire in others. There are always other ways to do the things that must be done. If we are creative, we will invent alternatives.

SIX WAYS IN WHICH CHILDREN AND ADOLESCENTS THINK DIFFERENTLY FROM ADULTS

If you paint with a broom, you're going to miss some spots. Drawing broad generalizations is like painting with a broom. Although the following six statements about how children think are generally true, there are exceptions to them. Some adults have these tendencies, just as some children don't.

1. Global versus specific statements: Children tend to make observations that are expressed as overstatements. The frustration of not doing well in a specific subject will be explained as "I'm a total loser." But in fact everybody has islands of competence; nobody is a total loser. Challenge potentially damaging self-understandings by helping students recognize evidence to the contrary. Provide them with examples of when they have performed well.

When challenging global statements, be specific and point out authentic competencies. Don't meet a negative generalization with a positive generalization. Remind the student of specific, recent successes. An example of how *not* to do this comes from the childhood of comedian Rodney Dangerfield. One day he returned home from school and told his father, "Dad, everybody hates me!" His father tried to comfort Rodney with "Don't say that, son. Everybody hasn't met you yet."

2. *Permanent versus temporary observations*: Children tend to conclude that an unpleasant temporary situation is a permanent condition. This creates the feeling that it is time to give up. Like the perpetually pessimistic Eeyore in *Winnie the Pooh,* children tend to ask, "What's the use?" Accumulated life experience teaches adults that most disappointments are temporary. Lacking life experience, children are vulnerable to believing that little Orphan Annie is wrong: the sun is *not* coming out tomorrow.

In his book *Learned Helplessness: A Theory for the Age of Personal Control* (Maier, Peterson, & Seligman 1995) psychologist Martin Seligman coined the term *learned helplessness* to describe the condition of people whose history of failure drives them to the conclusion that continuing effort will be futile. Dr. Seligman also believes that optimism can be taught. In his book, *Learned Optimism* (1990), he makes recommendations that imply several applications for teachers.

- Challenge a student's illogical conclusions and historical inaccuracies. Distorted thinking feeds Eeyore-like fatalism. Recovering alcoholics refer to illogical conclusions and factual inaccuracies as *stinking thinking*. It's especially helpful to remind a student of past success.
- Conduct *academic autopsies* in which you help a student analyze and understand why previous efforts produced undesirable results.
- Help a student construct other ways of doing things. (Remember what Ray Charles's mother said?) Inject some optimism into your student by explaining why you have confidence in the alternative the two of you have created.
- Assign accomplishable, intermediate tasks for your student so that incremental success can be experienced by reaching

modest goals. An analogy is the slumping baseball player who bunts the ball to build his confidence by making contact.

- Don't try to motivate students with an empty pep talk in which you encourage them to try harder. Students suffering from learned helplessness need a teacher, not a cheerleader. Even the most spirited pep talk will be ineffective unless it includes specific instruction.
- Don't give up on student. That amounts to giving them permission to quit.

3. External versus internal locus of control: As I noted in the chapter on motivation, children tend to explain their success and failure in terms of circumstances beyond their control or the actions of other people. Listen for indications of external locus of control mentality. You will be doing students a service whenever you emphasize how much they contribute to their own learning.

4. Immediate versus deferred gratification: Sigmund Freud summarized growing up as increasing ability to postpone gratification in favor of meeting responsibility. Perhaps the most significant difference between you, as an adult, and your students is in your greater ability to delay enjoyment. In your lesson planning, integrate activities your students will find enjoyable. However, be strategic in doing this, since nurturing your students' self-discipline is a part of their education.

5. Immediate and total versus process and partial: The difference between good and mediocre writers is their attitude toward their first draft. Children tend to approach work to "just get it done." Be patient with the student who accepts mediocrity with the age-appropriate statement, "That's good enough." Instead of reacting with "It's not good enough for me!" respond with "You're capable of doing better." While meeting deadlines is important, consider reinforcing the importance of quality by relaxing a deadline. *Immediate* ("That's good enough.") and *total* ("Just get it done!") thinking works against the student who would be better served by subdividing a project and carefully working through a process.

6. *Reactive versus reflective*: "Reactive thinking" is an oxymoron. The person who is reacting isn't thinking. It's been said that there's a world of difference between having to say something and having something to say. Driven by anxiety, children often react with unconsidered words. Reactions come from the gut; thinking comes from the head. The work of teaching includes patiently encouraging students to abandon the ineffective behavioral sequence of *ready . . . fire . . . aim!*

PARENT CONFERENCES

Meeting with the parents of your students is an important part of your work. Yet your teacher education courses likely devoted little or no attention to parent conferences. Harvard education professor Sara Lawrence-Lightfoot wrote a book about these meetings entitled *The Essential Conversation* (2003). Do you remember your parents going to your school's open house night? Didn't you anxiously await their return, meeting them at the door with the question, "What'd my teachers say about me?" What follows in this section are thoughts and suggestions that will help make your conversations with parents productive and substantial.

Don't take for granted that parents are comfortable meeting with teachers. Ideally, you will be engaged in a cooperative effort in the best interests of your students. However, your students' parents may have a history of unpleasant teacher conferences. Anticipate that parents will defend their children and may misperceive constructive criticism and relevant observations as attacks. If the parents themselves did poorly in school or had conflict with their teachers, they may not see schools as friendly places. In sports the home-field advantage is the favorable edge the home team enjoys over visitors. During parent conferences your familiarity with school gives you the home-field advantage. Unless you're meeting with parents who also are teachers, it's likely that you'll be more relaxed than they. Dr. Lawrence-Lightfoot (2003) refers to the history that both parents and teachers bring to a conference as the "ghosts in the room" (p. 3).

A hindrance to effective communication in all types of conversations occurs when the same words have different meanings for the parties involved. Teachers and parents want what is best for the child. However, sometimes what is best is understood differently. A dramatic example of this can be seen in the play *Inherit the Wind* (1960), in which a biology teacher is on trial for teaching Darwin's theory of natural selection. The story is set in a small, conservative town in the early 1900s. Believing it best for their children to be protected from ideas antagonistic to the Christian faith, the school board outlawed the teaching of Darwin's theory. Bertram Cates, the teacher, thought it best for his students to be exposed to this new idea. This is another area in which reaching for empathy may be helpful. If you are a parent, you are in a position to ask, "What would I want for my child?" (This is not to imply that you can't be an effective teacher unless you are a parent.)

A principle in the world of research is, *No data, no conclusion.* This is useful for teachers when discussing students. If you think something is true about a student, present it to parents as an impression, not a conclusion. Conclusions are supported only by documentation.

Another helpful research principle is, *Don't overgeneralize.* Overgeneralization occurs when too much is said from too little data. An illustration of this is the red-light syndrome. You've probably had the experience of stopping at a traffic light and thinking, "I always get this light!" The statistical fact is that you encounter that light green as often as red. It was the emotional surge of disappointment that moved you to overgeneralize. Documentation is the antidote for emotionally driven generalizations.

When meeting with parents, show them that you know their child and want to know him or her better. A particularly good question for communicating this is, *Is the child I'm describing familiar to you?* Also, ask parents about their child's strengths, talents, and interests.

It is the average student who is most likely to be overlooked by teachers. Teachers are familiar with both exceptional and struggling students. Students who have behavioral problems have a high profile with their teachers. It's the well-behaved, B-minus/C-plus student who often labors in obscurity.

Be sensitive to family and cultural differences that have an impact on your students. Family systems are disrupted by alcoholism, birth, death, cancer, divorce, depression, and unemployment. Parent conferences provide an opportunity to be current with your students' stressors and preoccupations. Trying to become familiar with a student's cultural heritage is not stereotyping. Culture is a part of everyone's story and contributes to uniqueness. Different cultures view and value education differently.

Through the years, teachers have communicated with parents using notes and telephone calls. In recent years e-mail has been added as a means of parental contact. As with all communication, take care in wording e-mails. There are no vocal cues in an e-mail, making warmth or subtle humor almost imperceptible. What is gained in frequency and immediacy with e-mail can be negated by coldness, unless each one is carefully crafted.

Finally, more than anything else, remember this: when it comes to their children, what parents least appreciate from teachers are surprises. Do the work of maintaining ongoing communication with parents.

LEARNING DISABILITIES

You are almost certain to work with learning-disabled students, even though you're not an expert on learning disabilities, and there are several things you need to know.

Learning-disabled students are those who perform substantially below what is expected for them given their age, grade, and measured intelligence. The term *learning disabled* is defined by exclusion. If a student's performance cannot be explained by a modality deficit (e.g., hearing loss), psychiatric condition (e.g., autism), personal trauma (e.g., parental divorce), physical trauma (e.g., head injury), or mental retardation (an IQ of less than seventy), then the term *learning disability* applies.

Learning-disabled students experience difficulties in any or several of the following operations:

- Receiving information (learning)
- Storing information (categorizing)
- Retrieving information (remembering)
- Speaking
- Listening
- Reading
- Writing
- Reasoning
- Doing mathematical problems

Learning-disabled students are in distinguished company. Albert Einstein, Thomas Edison, President Woodrow Wilson, and Tom Cruise are a few of the many accomplished people who overcame a learning disability. Since there are many ways of being intelligent, strengths can compensate for weaknesses.

If you're not familiar with the work of Richard Lavoie, become acquainted with his video presentation, *How Hard Can This Be?*

FAT City (1989). It will provide you with a quick study of learning disabilities in an informative and entertaining way. In fact every teacher, regardless of subject or grade level, should see it. Take advantage of conferences and in-service opportunities to learn more about learning disabilities. All of your students will benefit when you learn more about how people learn.

THE VALUE OF RESEARCH

If you've ever lost your keys or planned a trip, you've done research. Research is *the systematic gathering of information to answer a question, solve a problem, or address an issue.* In chapter 3, I pointed out that every significant educational topic has been subjected to research and writing. Further, becoming familiar and current with research that is relevant to your work will be your responsibility as a professional. In this sense, being a teacher is like being a lawyer. No lawyer can know everything about the law; the field is far too broad. Thus a lawyer must know how to research the law to locate answers and construct solutions and strategies. Similarly, no teacher can be an expert on all aspects of education. However, every teacher must be willing and able to find the experts and learn what they have to say.

Research is something you'll be doing to become informed of the research of others. But it might not be the only kind of research you'll be doing. Many master's and all doctoral degree programs require original research—an investigation intended to answer a question, solve a problem, or address an issue *for the first time.* This type of research adds something to the existing body of knowledge. If you accomplish original research, you'll be taking a place in a long line of individuals who have generated new information. If you publish your research, you'll be making your results available to others.

Does the thought of doing original research intimidate you? If so, consider that graduate programs requiring it include a course that teaches how to conduct and write research projects. A master's thesis may be described as a bar mitzvah for scholars. The work for elementary, secondary, and undergraduate students is to learn what is already known. If a master's program requires original research, then the graduate students must learn something previously unknown. In Judaism the bar mitzvah formalizes passage from childhood to adulthood. Similarly, the master's thesis marks the end of complete dependence on the research of others.

THE INFLUENCE OF CULTURE

Every year at least forty thousand people in the United States die from suicide. Immolation, setting oneself on fire, is a rare and deeply pathological method of self-destruction. Can you imagine a culture in which immolation is seen as reasonable and honorable? At least two such cultures have existed. Until it was outlawed in 1948, in the Indian ritual of *suttee*, a widow would throw herself onto the flames consuming her husband's body at his cremation. During the Vietnam War some Buddhist monks set themselves on fire in protest. How different can cultures be? They can be so different that not all of them view immolation as an expression of mental illness.

The word *culture* is one of those words people use regularly, but are hard-pressed to define. The United States is a nation. It is a geographical–political entity containing many cultures. When we speak of Native Americans, Japanese Americans, or African Americans we are referring to culture.

People from different cultures often see things differently, including education. In 1744 the College of William and Mary in

Virginia offered a free education to a dozen young men from the Indians of the Six Nations. In declining the offer, the chiefs of the Six Nations wrote to the college:

> We are convinc'd . . . that you mean to do us Good by your Proposal; and we thank you heartily. But you, who are wise, must know that different Nations have different Conceptions of things; and you will therefore not take it amiss, if our Ideas of this kind of Education happen not to be the same with yours. We have had some Experience of it. Several of our Young People were formerly brought up at the Colleges of the Northern Provinces . . . but, when they came back to us, they were . . . ignorant of every means of living in the Woods . . . spoke our Language imperfectly . . . [and] they were totally good for nothing. We are, however, not the less oblig'd by your kind Offer, tho' we decline accepting it; and to show our grateful Sense of it, if the Gentlemen of Virginia will send us a Dozen of their Sons, we will take care of their Education; instruct them in all we know, and make Men of them. (Carroll 1999, p. 335)

Do not assume that all Americans value education in the same way. The Amish believe that mastering the Three Rs (reading, 'riting, and 'rithmatic) is adequate schooling. In contrast, Asian families tend to value academic excellence and university education.

Also, be prepared for differences within a culture. To know a nonreligious Jewish person is not to know a Hasidic Jewish person. Familiarity with the Mohawk tribe does make you knowledgeable about other tribes. Stereotyping can result in an unpleasant collision of cultures.

STUDENT PSYCHOLOGICAL PROBLEMS

Of pornography it's been said, "I can't define it, but I know it when I see it." The same can be said about abnormal behavior.

You're a teacher, not a psychiatrist. Defining, diagnosing, and treating abnormal behavior will never be part of your job description. Recognizing and responding to it will be part of your work. It's almost certain that any behavior you will recognize as abnormal will have been noted already by parents and previous teachers. Nevertheless, report such behavior to your principal or vice principal. Reporting it will help you learn how to respond to the behavior in the best interest of all your students.

Abnormal or disordered behavior, also referred to as psychopathology, can be understood in terms of (1) *statistical abnormality*, in which a behavior occurs in less than 50% of a specified population, (2) *dysfunctional abnormality*, in which a behavior prevents or compromises a person's ability to accomplish appropriate tasks, and (3) *distressful abnormality*, in which individuals are troubled by their own behavior. Applying these descriptions to your work implies several things. First, it will mean not overreacting to a behavior that is rarely seen. People sometimes behave in ways that are statistically abnormal or even eccentric, but not pathological. Second, it will mean being primarily concerned with your student's ability to accomplish appropriate tasks. Third, it will mean considering that the behavior that bothers you also troubles the student.

The following principles are helpful when you are working with students who have psychological issues:

- Anticipate and respect that mental health professionals must maintain client–therapist confidentiality. Many of these professionals refuse to meet with teachers. Other therapists do not discuss anything from a therapy session, unless the client has given permission to do so. It is appropriate to ask therapists for specific suggestions they have for teachers. You might find it effective for you to frame your concerns as *what if* questions and a request for things for you to do and things for you not to do.

- Remember that your obligation to a troubled student is the same as your obligation to all other students.
- Don't extend confidentiality to a student without first knowing the secret you'll be keeping. Don't sign a blank check. Student safety surpasses all other concerns. Point out to students who insist on confidentiality first that they have an obvious need to talk about something very important.
- Don't be an amateur psychiatrist. In fact, *amateur psychiatrist* is an oxymoron. Diagnosis and treatment are matters for professionals. Don't accept a diagnosis of a student unless it was made by a mental health professional.
- Investigate behaviors you've noted as abnormal. Talk to the student's previous teachers as well as his or her parents. In these conversations report your observations without suggesting a diagnosis or making a judgment. Before meeting, be clear in your own mind as to what you want to learn and ask questions that will enable you to learn it.
- As emphasized earlier, you are not a mental health professional. Nevertheless, it might be helpful if you become familiar with the psychological problems you're likely to encounter as a teacher of adolescents. The following is a list of these problems.

1. Asperger's disorder
2. Attention deficit/hyperactivity disorder
3. Depression
4. Eating disorders (anorexia nervosa, bulimia nervosa, obesity)
5. Learning disabilities
6. Oppositional defiant disorder
7. Self-mutilation (cutting)

8. Social anxiety
9. Substance abuse
10. Suicidality

- Dawna Buchanan, a Missouri teacher, has observed, "Sometimes it seems my most difficult students teach me the most—about patience, listening, compassion, trying harder, and tolerance" (Kelly-Gangi and Patterson 2001, p. 82). If you work with students in their best interest, you will find that no virtue will serve them and you as well as patience.

CRITICISM: HOW TO GIVE AND RECEIVE IT

We know the feeling. It comes full circle and suddenly we realize we've made a serious mistake. A neurologist could describe what happens to the central nervous system at the moment of realization when "Oh no!" or something less delicate explodes from our mouths. I had such a moment twenty-five years ago when, after several minutes of studying a large displayed map at a Pennsylvania Turnpike rest stop, the inescapable conclusion was that I had been driving in the wrong direction for an hour. "Paulette," I said to my sister-in-law, "we've been going west instead of north for sixty miles."

"I know," she replied calmly. "You took a wrong turn coming out of Philadelphia."

"What!" I exclaimed incredulously. "You saw me take a wrong turn and didn't say anything?"

"Yes," she replied with no hint of defensiveness. "I thought of saying something, but I know you don't handle criticism well, so I thought it would be better if you realized it on your own."

It didn't take long for my anger to turn to disappointment. "What kind of person am I to Paulette," I wondered, "that she would prefer traveling sixty miles in the wrong direction to confronting me with my undeniable mistake?'"

The word *criticism* is derived from the Greek word *criterion*: a means for making judgments. Unfortunately, too often the criticisms we receive are not objective. Instead, they are driven by the critic's taste or irritation at some inconvenience. Teachers are leaders and leaders affect the lives of people. Whoever makes a decision or takes an action that affects others is available for criticism.

It's traditional wisdom that it is more blessed to give than receive. Criticism, if not blessed, is more easily given than received. Teaching involves both giving and receiving criticism. What follows are principles for doing both.

RECEIVING CRITICISM

1. Much criticism is like junk mail, addressed to "occupant," which means no one in particular. It's not unusual for criticism to be directed toward teachers, since they are available representatives of a school, school district, or profession. Although unpleasant, such criticism will be less provocative if you recognize that it's unrelated to anything you have or haven't done.

2. Some criticism results from the mood of the critic. This is another instance of criticism unrelated to your performance.

3. Valid criticism can be recognized as convergent data. When you hear the same criticism from several people who don't know each other, consider this convergent data and take it seriously.

4. Since anger drives a lot of criticism, it's not unusual for criticism to be hyperbolic. Rather than dismiss purposefully

overstated criticism, observe the kernel-of-truth principle. Consider if any truth, however small, lies in the exaggeration.

5. Don't immediately dismiss a criticism because of the messenger. True, it is important to consider the source. But even a blind squirrel finds a nut.

6. You are responsible for the intentions and effects of your actions. Saying, "I didn't mean for that to happen," does not relieve you of responsibility for unintended results. A responsible person anticipates and accounts for all predictable consequences of an action. Ready . . . fire! . . . aim is an indefensible action sequence.

7. When receiving criticism, take responsibility for things you've actually said or done. You are not responsible for what someone has imagined you've done or predicted you'd do. Neither are you accountable for untrue motives assigned to you. Never are you responsible for what you've done in someone's dreams.

8. Have a balanced attitude toward criticism. Somewhere between rejecting criticism and being devastated by it is the ability to consider and profit from it. Kipling (1993) wrote, "If all men count with you, but none too much." Presidents shouldn't be ruled by approval ratings and polls, but neither should they disregard them. Reflect on criticism in the context of your overall mission as a teacher. But do not abandon and redefine your calling because of an unfavorable evaluation. Morrie Schwartz, the professor featured in Mitch Albom's *Tuesdays with Morrie* (1997), was criticized by some students for not being a scholar. Morrie's agenda in his teaching did not include presenting himself as a learned and erudite lecturer. He acknowledged the criticism without reordering his carefully considered approach to teaching.

9. In Sonya Friedman's *On a Clear Day, You Can See Yourself* (1991), she affirms that it is a myth that you can please

everyone if you work diligently at doing so. If you read movie and book reviews, you'll be impressed by the range of evaluations. One critic applauds what another berates. Be prepared for mixed reviews from students, parents, colleagues, and administrators.

GIVING CRITICISM

1. Giving criticism is a delicate operation. Like organ transplant surgery, it involves giving something helpful to the recipient if it's not rejected. In transplantation the recipient's body identifies the new organ as something foreign and therefore threatening. When offering criticism, be mindful that you are introducing something uninvited that a student could mistake as harmful. Like a skilled surgeon concerned with rejection, proceed with care.

2. Common experiences generate empathy. You've had the experience of receiving criticism. Use that experience to plan your delivery. The student you criticize has a history that includes previous criticism. Often the past merges with the present. If there's an overreaction, consider the possibility that it is being driven by something in the student's history.

3. Criticism is always received personally. It's laughable when a criticism is preceded by the qualifying phrase, "Please don't take this personally." Carefully consider your introduction. Before giving a criticism, consider the student's personality, especially the characteristics of resiliency and fragility. Circumstantial variables to weigh are time, place, and the need for privacy.

4. Rarely is criticism given to a stranger. Evaluate your history with the student. Ask yourself if it's a history that includes

encouragement and affirmation. If every prior communication with a student involved a criticism, consider that you might not be the best person for delivering yet another negative evaluation. If you have to be that person, redouble your determination to be tactful and patient.

5. As much as you can, frame the criticism in positive terms. *Constructive criticism* is not an oxymoron. Speak optimistically of the future, using phrases like "Something that will work better for you the next time is . . . " and "What you did is understandable, but in the future it would be better if you . . . " Richard Lavoie (1994), an expert on learning disabled children, coined the phrase "behavioral autopsies" for his redemptive postmisbehavioral debriefings with students.

6. Reacting and reflecting are not synonymous. Reactions come from the gut and are not preceded by thought. Reflections come from the head—the products of deliberation. Do not criticize reactively, according to your mood. Any form of discipline driven by mood will be inconsistent, indefensible, and confusing to the students.

7. Giving criticism and insulting are not the same. If you catch yourself saying, "You're lazy!" then you're insulting, not constructively criticizing. Criticism is most likely to be effective when it addresses a specific behavior. Similar to insulting, and also ineffective, is estimating motivation. If you catch yourself saying, "You did that because . . . " then you're engaged in mind reading, not productive criticism.

However justified you feel when insulting or assigning motivation, it almost never contributes to anything good. It is possible to be right but still ineffective. The goal is to be helpful, not factually correct. Words and actions that erode a relationship with a student will not lead to a desirable result.

8. Make a conscious effort not to use the phrase, "If I were you . . . " While it's presented as a hypothetical construction, it could be received as "I am better than you." Besides, phrases like "If I were you" and "If you were me" are meaningless. When someone asks me, "If you were me, what would you do?" I respond with "If I were you, then I'd do what you would do, *because I'd be you!*" (An alternative response is "I don't know what I'd do because I wouldn't exist and wouldn't be having this conversation.")

Teaching requires criticizing students. It's not a question of whether or not you'll be making evaluations. It's a question of whether or not your evaluations will be valid and helpful.

As for receiving criticism, President Harry Truman is credited with saying, "If you can't stand the heat, get out of the kitchen." You don't have to be the president of the United States to be the target of criticism. How you manage criticism will determine whether or not it makes you a more effective teacher and, more importantly, a person who seeks improvement.

TEACHING CONTROVERSIAL ISSUES

While this book was being written, a forty-one-year-old brain-damaged woman, Terri Schiavo, was euthanized. The removal of her feeding tube was disputed in legal, medical, and philosophical circles. Controversial issues provide rich and exciting opportunities for instructing students in formulating defensible opinions and, perhaps, locating truth. Potentially each edition of the daily newspaper provides material for constructivist and cooperative learning. Teachers who show that they have weighed and measured alternative points of view are encouraging their students to do the same, in matters academic as well as personal.

The following questions will help you organize your thinking about the teaching of controversial issues: (1) What is the nature of controversy? (2) How does a teacher determine when to engage students in a controversial issue? (3) How are teachers to conduct themselves when teaching a controversial issue?

A controversy exists when (1) a strong intellectual argument can be made for two or more opposing positions, and (2) the issue in dispute involves two or more parties with equal and competing interests. Oscar Wilde is reputed to have defined dilemmas as situations in which no matter what you choose, you are wrong. When good men on both sides of an issue disagree, a controversy exists.

How does a teacher determine when to engage students in a controversial issue? Shakespeare wrote, "Beware of entrance to a quarrel, but being in, bear that the opposed may beware of thee" (*Hamlet* 1.3.65–68). Determining the appropriateness of a controversial issue for a class requires the consideration of several questions.

To whom is the issue important? Among whom is the controversy being disputed? Appearance to the contrary, these are two different questions. In the case of Mrs. Schiavo, the controversial issue was important to her family and the medical and legal personnel directly involved in her case. However, the disputing parties included countless individuals interested in the social, political, and legal ramifications of the decision concerning her feeding tube. Media coverage showed support for and opposition to her euthanasia among lawyers, doctors, politicians, talk show personalities, and citizens at large.

What is the topic of the controversy? A suggested sequence for the clarification of a research proposal is *topic, problem,* and *rationale* (Booth, Colomb, and Williams 1995). The topic is the subject of the problem to be investigated. The rationale is the reason(s) why the research would have significant value. To return to the illustration provided by Terri Schiavo, the problem was whether or not to remove her feeding tube. The topic of this controversy was euthanasia. The rationale included that her case was not unique and could provide a legal precedent. The next two questions establish the necessity of identifying the controversy's topic.

Before a controversial issue is taught, the subject of the controversy must be identified. Once identified, this is the question to be answered: *Is this topic a part of the course curriculum?* The answer to this question could provide reassurance that the subject is appropriate for the class. Since courses have objectives as well as content, a second question must be answered: Would engagement in this topic contribute to this course's stated objectives for these students? The answer to this question could provide reassurance that consideration of the topic is compatible with the desired learning outcomes for the students. In the case of Mrs. Schiavo, consideration of the complexity of the issue could nurture students in the development of critical thinking ability. Also, engagement in this issue could include a discussion of how to appropriately respond to a point of view one finds disagreeable.

How are teachers to conduct themselves when teaching a controversial issue? After it has been determined that including a controversial issue in a course can be defended in terms of its content and objectives, the teacher must then be concerned with pedagogy. Teaching controversial issues is no different from any other category of instruction. All teaching should be conducted with authenticity and integrity.

To consider authenticity's opposite characteristic, phoniness, is to recognize authenticity as a virtue. Shakespeare's instruction to "assume a virtue if you have it not" cannot apply to authenticity (*Hamlet* 3.4.161). *Feigned authenticity* is an oxymoron. It is dishonest for a teacher to have a position on a controversial issue and claim otherwise. Further, it is an insult to students. It is implying to them, "You can't handle the truth!" (Sorkin 1991).

The teacher who admits having a position on a disputed matter but refuses to share it is being authentic, but no less insulting. It implies that the teacher's influence is too strong for the students to resist. There is a hint of arrogance in the assumption that if students are privy to a teacher's opinion the students will embrace it *because* the teacher holds it.

The word *integrity* means wholeness. Giving the strongest possible representation of both sides of an issue is to teach with integrity. Teachers who share the process by which a conclusion has been reached are teaching with integrity. In the teaching of controversial issues, responsible pedagogy often requires teachers to make a conscientious effort to present a point of view with which they disagree. Like a jury trial, two strong arguments are to be made. Unlike a jury trial, one person represents both sides. And unlike a jury trial, one presenter addresses the perceived weaknesses of both arguments. It would be pedagogical malpractice for a teacher to do any less than the work of two opposing attorneys.

Nurturing authenticity and integrity in students encourages them in the acquisition of a life skill that will benefit them beyond the classroom. As a teacher, you will have opportunities to model that having a carefully considered opinion does not preclude conceding that there is strength in the opposing position. Further, being able to articulate the process by which an opposing point of view was reached is a demonstration of how to show respect in an interpersonal conflict by making an effort to understand the other person.

9

EPILOGUE

Teachers believe they have a gift for giving; it drives them with the same irrepressible drive that drives others to create a work of art or a market or a building.

—A. Bartlett Giamatti

A. Bartlett Giamatti had a career that took him from one passion to another to another—teacher, president of Yale University, and then commissioner of major league baseball. Giamatti demonstrated the irrepressible drive to give. If you believe you have a gift for giving, then you're in a position to believe in yourself as a teacher. Effective teachers carry on their work confident in the belief that they are contributing to something valuable. These teachers are driven by the conviction that being a part of the intellectual and character development of young people is a high calling.

Two other characteristics of effective teachers are optimism and self-discipline. Optimism is an attitude. Clergyman Charles Swindoll (1982) has estimated that attitude accounts for 90% of life's events.

The longer I live, the more I realize that impact of attitude on my life. Attitude, to me, is more important than facts. It is more important than education, than money, than circumstances, than failure, than successes, than what other people think or say or do. It is more important than appearance, giftedness or skill. It will make or break a company . . . a church . . . a home. The remarkable thing is we have a choice every day regarding the attitude we will embrace for that day. We cannot change our past . . . [and] we cannot change the fact that people will act in a certain way. We cannot change the inevitable. The only thing we can do is play on the one string that we have, and that is our attitude. I am convinced that life is 10% what happens to me and 90% how I react to it. And so it is with you . . . . [W]e are in charge of our attitudes. (p. 12)

One of the most popular self-help books ever written is *The Road Less Traveled* by Scott Peck (1978). It begins with three words, "Life is difficult." The remainder of the book is Dr. Peck's instruction that self-discipline is the characteristic required for successfully responding to the innumerable challenges that make life difficult. Self-discipline is necessary for wise and efficient time management. Effective teachers know the value of being skillful at using time optimally. In *How to Live on Twenty-Four Hours a Day*, Arnold Bennett (2000) provides the philosophy of time that proved helpful in his life.

Time is the inexplicable raw material of everything. With it, all is possible; without it, nothing. The supply of time is truly a daily miracle, an affair genuinely astonishing when one examines it.

You wake up every morning, and lo! your purse is magically filled with twenty-four hours of the unmanufactured tissue of your life! It is yours. It is the most precious of possessions. . . . No one can take it from you. It is unstealable. And no one receives either more or less than you receive.

In the realm of time there is no aristocracy of wealth, and no aristocracy of intellect. Genius is never rewarded by even an extra hour a day. And there is no punishment. Waste your infinitely precious commodity as much as you will, and the supply will never be withheld from you. . . . Moreover, you cannot draw upon the future. Impossible to get into debt! You can only waste the passing moment. You cannot waste tomorrow; it is kept for you. I have said the affair is a miracle. Is it not? (pp. 2–3)

REFERENCES

Albom, M. 1997. *Tuesdays with Morrie: An Old Man, Young Man, and Life's Greatest Lesson.* New York: Doubleday.

Associated Press. 2003. *First Public Gay High School to Open in NYC.* Retrieved August 13, 2005, from http://www.cnn.com/2003/education/07/28/gay.school.ap.

Bennett, A. 2000. *How to Live on Twenty-Four Hours a Day.* Hyattsville, Md.: Shambling Gate.

Bennett, W. 1993. *The Book of Virtues.* New York: Simon & Schuster.

Bluestein, J. 2001. *Creating Emotionally Safe Schools: A Guide for Educators and Parents.* Deerfield Beach, Fla.: Health Communications.

Booth, W., Colomb, G., and Williams, J. 1995. *The Craft of Research.* Chicago: University of Chicago Press.

Buscaglia, L. 1989. *Papa.* New York: Morrow.

Card, H. 1998. *The Poetry of Teaching.* Syracuse, N.Y.: Thornetree Hill Poetry Press.

Carroll, A., ed. 1999. *Letters of a Nation: A Collection of Extraordinary American Letters.* New York: Random House.

Cohen, R. 2004. *Blindsided.* New York: HarperCollins.

Coles, J. R. 1995. "The Disparity Between Intellect and Character." *Chronicle of Higher Education, 40*(3): A-68.

Dead Poets Society. 1989. Touchstone Home Video. 128 minutes.

Esquith, R. (2003). *There Are No Shortcuts.* New York: Pantheon.

Fowler, J. W. 1981. *Stages of Faith: The Psychology of Human Development and Quest for Meaning.* New York: HarperCollins.

Friedman, S. 1991. *On a Clear Day, You Can See Yourself: Turning the Life You Have Into the Life You Want.* New York: Random House.

Fulghum, R. 2003. *All I Really Need to Know I Learned in Kindergarten.* New York: Ballantine. Originally printed in 1988.

Funder, D. 1997. *The Personality Puzzle.* New York: Norton.

Garbarino, J. 1997, April. "Educating Children in a Toxic Environment." *Educational Leadership, 54*(7): 12–16.

Gardner, H. 1983. *Frames of Mind: The Theory of Multiple Intelligences.* New York: Basic Books.

Gardner, H. 1999. "Are There Additional Intelligences?" In J. Kane (Ed.), *Education, Information, and Transformation: Essays on Learning and Thinking* (pp. 111–113). Upper Saddle River, NJ: Prentice-Hall.

Gates, W. 1998. "Charity Begins When I'm Ready." Retrieved December 27, 2005, from http://www.fortune.com/fortune/print/0, 15935, 1117906, 00 .htm.

Greene, R. 2000. *The Explosive Child: A New Approach for Understanding and Parenting Easily Frustrated, Chronically Inflexible Children.* New York: Harper Collins.

Hample, S., and Marshal, E. 1991. *Children's Letters to God.* New York: Workman.

Hoffer, E. 1983. *Truth Imagined.* New York: Harper & Row.

Horowitz, J. 2003. "Ten Foods That Pack a Wallop." *Time, 159*(3), January 21: 50–55.

Inherit the Wind. 1960. MGM Studios. 128 minutes.

John F. Kennedy Library and Museum. 2005. *Address of Senator John F. Kennedy Accepting the Democratic Party Nomination for Presidency of the United States.* Retrieved August 13, 2005, from http://www.jfklibrary.org/ j071560.htm.

Kelly-Gangi, C., and Patterson, J. 2001. *Celebrating Teachers.* New York: Barnes & Noble Books.

Kipling, R. 1993. "If." *The Book of Virtues*, edited by William Bennett, 476–77. New York: Simon & Schuster.

Kohn, A. 1993. "Rewards Versus Learning: A Response to Paul Chance." *Phi Delta Kappan,* June, 74, 783–87.

Lakoff, G., and Johnson, M. 1980. *Metaphors We Live By.* Chicago: University of Chicago Press.

Lavoie, R. 1989. *How Hard Can This Be? FAT City.* PBS Videos. 40 minues.

Lavoie, R. 1994. *Learning Disabilities and Social Skills: The Last One Picked . . . The First One Picked On.* Washington, D.C.: WETA-TV. 62 minutes.

Lawrence-Lightfoot, S. 2003. *The Essential Conversation: What Parents and Teachers Can Learn From Each Other.* New York: Random House.

Lederer, R. 2005. *Revenge of Anguished English: More Accidental Assaults Upon Our Language.* New York: St. Martin's Press.

Ludewig, L. 1994. "Students, Professors Point Out Each Other's Irritating Behaviors." In P. Vogt (Ed.), *Recruitment and Retention,* 8(7).

Maier, S., Peterson, C., and Seligman, M. 1995. *Learned Helplessness: A Theory for the Age of Personal Control.* New York: Knopf.

Malikow, M. 2005, Summer. "Pedagogical Autopsies: Constructively Reflecting on a Lesson That Died." *New Teacher Advocate. Kappa Delta Pi.*

Moore, E. 2000. "Why Teachers Are Not 'Those Who Can't.'" *Newsweek,* April 3, 13.

Peck, S. 1978. *The Road Less Traveled.* New York: Simon & Schuster.

Pipher, M. 1994. *Reviving Ophelia.* New York: Ballantine.

Powell, C. 2002. "Leadership Primer." In *The Leadership Secrets of Colin Powell* (p. 236). New York: McGraw-Hill.

The Princess Diaries. 2001. Brown House Products/Bottom of Ninth Productions, Inc./Walt Disney Pictures. 110 minutes.

Rand, A. 1961. *The Virtue of Selfishness.* New York: Penguin Books.

Reilly, R. 2003a. "Extreme Measures." *Sports Illustrated,* May 19, p. 154.

Reilly, R. 2003b. "Worth the Wait." *Sports Illustrated,* October 20, p. 154.

Rogers, C. 1969. *Freedom to Learn.* Columbus, Ohio: Merrill.

Seligman, M. 1990. *Learned Optimism: How to Change Your Mind and Your Life.* New York: Simon & Schuster.

Selzer, R. 1977. *Mortal Lessons: Notes on the "Art of Surgery."* Orlando, Fla.: Harcourt Brace.

Selzer, R. 1982. *Letters to a Young Doctor.* New York: Simon & Schuster.

Sorkin, A. 1991. *A Few Good Men.* Columbia Tri-Star.

Swindoll, C. 1982. *Strengthening Your Grip.* Dallas, Tex.: Word.

Szasz, T. 1873. *The Second Sin: Some Iconoclastic Thoughts on Marriage, Sex, Drugs, Mental Illness, and Other Matters.* Garden City, NY: Anchor Press.

Woolfolk, A. 2004. *Educational Psychology.* Boston: Allyn & Bacon.

Zajonc, R. B. 1984. "Rethinking I.Q. Tests and Their Value." *New York Times,* July 22, D22.

ABOUT THE AUTHOR

Max Malikow, Th.D., is an assistant professor of education at Le Moyne College in Syracuse, New York, and an adjunct professor of psychology at Syracuse University and the Crouse Hospital School of Nursing. His teaching career includes twenty years in secondary education as a social studies teacher. He coauthored *Living When a Young Friend Commits Suicide* and has written numerous scholarly publications. He is also a psychotherapist in private practice.